ART STAMPING
WORKSHOP

CREATE HAND-CARVED STAMPS FOR UNIQUE PROJECTS ON PAPER, FABRIC, POLYMER CLAY AND MORE

NORTH LIGHT BOOKS
CINCINNATI, OHIO
...network.com

GLORIA PAGE

CARVING BY STEPHANIE CHAO

10 09 08 07 06   5 4 3 2 1

Distributed in Canada by Fraser Direct

100 Armstrong Avenue

Georgetown, ON, Canada L7G 5S4

Tel: (905) 877-4411

Distributed in the U.K. and Europe by David & Charles

Brunel House, Newton Abbot, Devon, TQ12 4PU, England

Tel: (+44) 1626 323200, Fax: (+44) 1626 323319

Email: mail@davidandcharles.co.uk

Distributed in Australia by Capricorn Link

P.O. Box 704, S. Windsor, NSW 2756 Australia

Tel: (02) 4577-3555

Library of Congress Cataloging-in-Publication Data

Page, Gloria.

   Art stamping workshop : create hand-carved stamps for unique projects on paper, fabric, polymer clay and more! / Gloria Page.-- 1st ed.

      p. cm.

   Includes index.

   ISBN 1-58180-696-5 (pbk. : alk. paper)

   1. Handicraft. 2. Block printing. I. Title.

   TT857.P35 2006

   761--dc22

                    2005013705

Editor: Tonia Davenport
Cover Designer: Brian Roeth
Designer: Marissa Bowers
Photo Stylist: Jan Nickum
Layout Artist: Jessica Schultz
Production Coordinator: Robin Richie
Photographers: Tim Grondin, Al Parrish and Hal Barkan

fw
F+W PUBLICATIONS, INC.

ABOUT THE AUTHOR

GLORIA PAGE is a wife, Mom, artist, author and teacher. Her artistic life is a wide horizon of interests, which started when she was a child. The world of stamping opened up new doors and launched a business beyond the hobby when she started Impressions Art Designs in 1993. Since then, Gloria has made and sold tens of thousands of hand-made cards and other art pieces. Her greeting card account with the Smithsonian has been active for many years. From juried art shows to galleries, from teaching stamping and carving in different venues including a university craft studio, to writing a book of her business memoirs, Gloria pursues her creative dreams.

Her extensive work and writing is published in magazines such as *Somerset Studio, Belle Armoire* and many art publications and books.

In this book, Gloria shares her carving and stamping techniques and invites her carving art friends to share their inspiring work in an extensive Gallery section. This book is the culmination of years of artistic exploration and it is also the beginning of more to come.

To learn more about Gloria, visit:
www.impressionsart.com

DEDICATION • DEDICATION • DEDICATION • DEDICATION • DEDICATION • DEDICATION • DEDICATION • DEDICATION • DEDICATION

**TO MY HUSBAND, GARY,
AND OUR TWO CHILDREN, BRANDON AND BRYAN.**

DEDICATION • DEDICATION • DEDICATION • DEDICATION • DEDICATION • DEDICATION • DEDICATION • DEDICA

ACKNOWLEDGMENTS • ACKNOWLEDGMENTS • ACKNOWLEDGMENTS • ACKNOWLEDGMENTS • ACKNOWLEDGMENTS • ACKNOWLEDGMEN

Sharilyn Miller, mentor and friend, opened this door for me with a question: "So, Gloria, when are you going to do *your* how-to book?" For her encouraging push and all the guidance along the way, I am so grateful.

Many thanks go to my family and friends for their support and cheering over the years! To Julie Hagan Bloch and Luann Udell, for their friendship, loving support, laughter, and the blessing to go ahead and do my own carving book. (They are my carving teachers.) To all carving friends who shared their experiences, techniques and tricks of the trade with me over the years—your insights are woven in here and I thank you all.

To Tricia Waddell at North Light Books for believing in this book and in me. To my editor, Tonia, and my photo-shoot photographer, Tim, for the great time we had and the expertise and vision they brought to this project. To the North Light team who produced this book—those I had the privilege to meet and those behind the scenes—I am very grateful and honored.

To all the artists who contributed such beautiful artwork—I wish we had room for every single piece! You are all appreciated. The Gallery is so inspiring! To my many artist friends whose ideas, humor, shared techniques and generosity along the way helped to make me a better artist and this book a better book—thank you so much.

To the readers of this book, whether new to carving or master carvers—**LET'S CARVE AND BE CREATIVE TOGETHER!**

ACKNOWLEDGMENTS • ACKNOWLEDGMENTS • ACKNOWLEDGMENTS • ACKNOWLEDGMENTS • ACKNOWLEDGMENTS • ACKNOWLEDGMENTS • ACKNOWLEDGMENTS • ACKNOWLEDGMENTS • ACKNOWLEDGMENTS • ACKNOWLEDGMENTS • ACKNOWLEDGMENTS • ACKNOWLE

TABLE OF CONTENTS

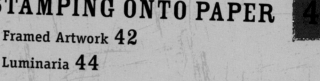

STAMPING ONTO PAPER · 40

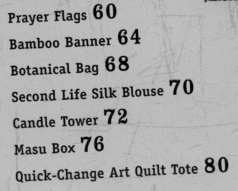

STAMPING ONTO FABRIC · 58

ALTERNATIVE SURFACES 84

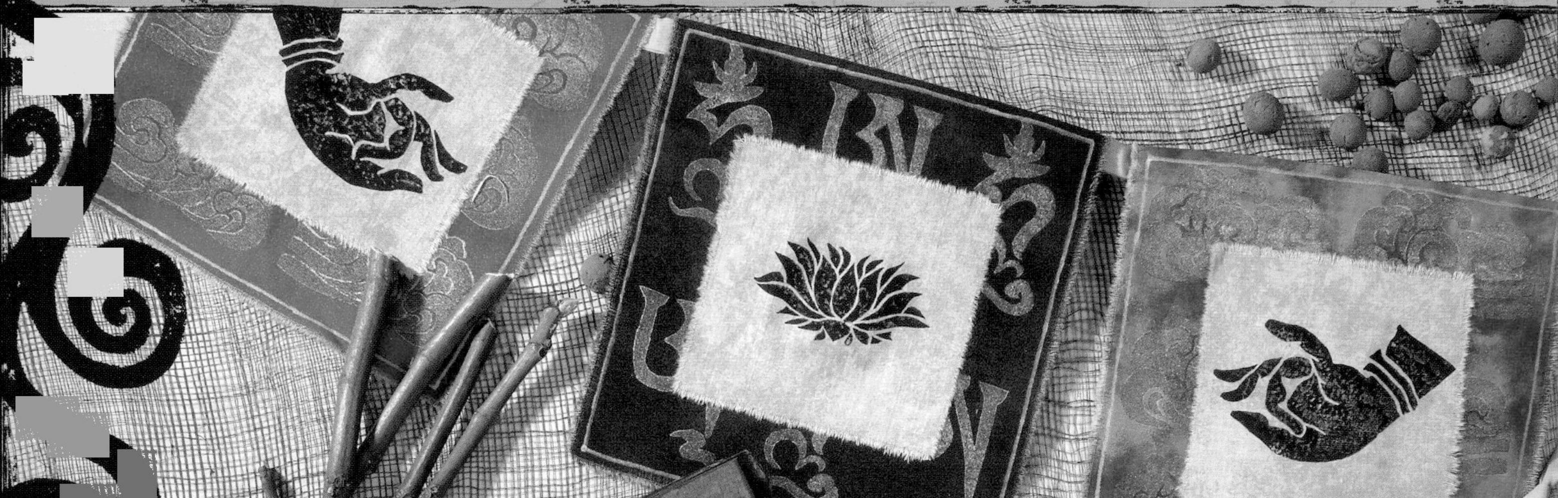

INTRODUCTION

IMAGINE . . . you are working on an art project, and you have a great idea. You need a particular image that can be stamped. There is only one problem: You don't have a stamp of that image and you want one—*now*! Enter the wonderful world of carving—you take out a piece of carving material, get your idea down on paper and create your very own stamp. A creative freedom and satisfaction comes to those who try this wonderful art form. Welcome to the club!

You need a little square stamp to finish off a card? Carve it! You want a huge spiral for a fabric piece? Carve it! For your altered book, you want a unique alphabet that no one else has ever seen? Draw it and carve it! Scrapbooking frames all start to look the same, so why not carve your own?

From a versatile shadow stamp to a poster-sized piece, each stamp is an art tool that can find infinite outlets. From the simplest shape to a complex portrait, it all starts with very simple techniques and inexpensive tools. Whatever art medium you work with, my very good guess is that gaining a mastery of even the most basic techniques explored in this book will open up new forms of expression in your art.

In 1993, my husband gave me my first art stamp and showed me how to use it; thank you, Gary! I made price tags for miniature grapevine wreaths with it. Next, three Southwest stamps from my Mom launched what would quickly become a handmade bookmark and card business. Then, an order from a gallery in Madrid, New Mexico, put me in a quandary: I needed a stamp of a picket fence and it had to be a certain size. It also needed to be "funky," not sweet and pristine. None of my catalogs came through for me. I needed help!

In a rubber stamp magazine, I had seen an ad for a little book whose title had stuck with me: *Carving Stamps* and something about "eraser carving . . ." (Thank you, Julie Hagan Bloch.) I made a fateful decision: Because I couldn't find a picket fence to suit my needs, darn it, I was going to carve one myself. I went out and bought an eraser—a chunky gum eraser. I had a craft knife around and figured that might do it, so I got started. I drew directly on the eraser (I had no clue that there were other options) and carved my very first stamp: "Picket Fence" by Gloria Page.

There was something so wonderful about solving that first dilemma, and I hope my book inspires you to just go ahead and do it, too. I'll always remember inking up that funny little rough image, printing it, lifting up and seeing what I had created. The eraser is a bit crumbly and the lines are pretty messy, but if you have ever visited very cool Madrid, New Mexico, you know that "the look" definitely works! I made and sold many bookmarks using that fence. It was a beginning.

Over time, different terms have come to be used for this art form. *Carving and printing soft blocks* is the current terminology, and at the same time we can say *carving our own stamps, eraser carving*, or whatever you like to call it. We are talking about basically the same thing, and I can guarantee that there will be a wonderful continuation in the evolution of terms and techniques.

In this book, I want to introduce you to my personal approach to carving stamps. I will share ideas and introduce projects that will make great gifts, home décor, personal apparel and accessories and, if you are into having your own art business on whatever level, products for you to sell. Many of the projects here are items that I have sold over the years in my own art business. Take the ideas, add your own signature to them, and have fun, make money, make people happy and, best of all, gain a hobby and an art skill that can provide you with much artful peace and satisfaction. Now, a word of caution: Carving can be addictive! And that is a wonderful thing. Imagine the possibilities! Better yet?

CARVE THE POSSIBILITIES . . .

IMAGE INSPIRATION

"OKAY, SO WHAT AM I GOING TO CARVE ANYWAY? I NEED AN IDEA—AN IMAGE ... SO NOW WHAT?" HERE ARE SOME IDEAS TO GET YOU STARTED.

"A thousand-mile journey begins with one step."

CHINESE PROVERB

DRAWING AND DOODLING

There are times when you have a very specific need. You might say, "I need a leaf stamp to make a border. 'Leaf' is the idea—now what?" You can draw one. ("Draw one?" some of you might be whispering with a certain panicked glaze over your eyes.) Yes, you can draw one! I have loved stamping for many reasons, one of them being that I previously did not have any confidence in my ability to draw, but carving my own stamps took care of that little insecurity quite nicely.

Over time, I found there wasn't always the "leaf of my dreams" available as a reference in a magazine or book, so I tried drawing very simple ones and liked them! The spirals I wanted were more "doodly," so I doodled and drew some that worked very well. How hard could it be to draw a heart? I gave it a try and really liked the way it turned out. I have a thing for images of hands, so I traced my right hand and added a spiral inside—very cool! I broke through the resistance to drawing my own designs by the only means I know: I just did it.

Once I started carving, the print-making aspect of stamping freed up my thinking. As I altered existing designs, I realized that I was "drawing" new elements. It was a beginning. Can you draw? Can you doodle? If you *want* to, the answer is yes—so have fun giving it a try! Kids do this stuff all the time. Why not take advantage of the child inside of you?

BOOKS AND MAGAZINES

Whenever there is a discussion about getting images to work with, you can be sure someone will always raise a hand and say, "Dover royalty-free books!" And they are right to be enthusiastic. I have a large collection of them. When I was in the handmade card business full-time, with more than fifty active accounts, most of my business was making Southwestern- and Asian-style cards. Because many of my accounts were museum shops, I wanted to use images that were authentic. I enlarged images I found in those books and carved them.

I would like to share the way I view designs in Dover books or anything in print. I look at the design as a whole, and I also study the design in smaller parts. Let's say that I need a strong African-style image for a fabric piece. The Dover book *African Designs from Traditional Sources* is one of my all-time favorites. A design jumps out at me. I study it. Would it be complicated to carve? Is there a repetitive element in the design that I can single out to make the carving easier? One design in the book might have many triangles, but if I carve just one triangle, I can stamp it many times and reproduce the same look easily.

Look at the individual parts of a design. If something looks beyond your carving ability at the moment, see if you can simplify it and break it down. In doing so, you personalize it at the same time. There was a particular African stamp I once carved, whose original design included many tiny dots. There was no way that I was going to carve out all those teeny tiny little things! However, I knew with a pen or marker, I could add them later if I wanted to. If you aren't stuck on being too literal, you will find your personal expression developing along with your carving ability.

HOUSEHOLD AND STUDIO THINGS

Image inspirations are everywhere, really. I have some very old placemats that I just love. Four are fabric and one is paper. I have made carvings of their designs after tracing directly over them using tracing paper. If I wanted to enlarge or shrink the image, I could photocopy the tracing and size it up or down.

Do you love Mexican and Italian tiles? Carve a tile's design based on what you see. Look at the individual elements in the design. What about flooring? It can be very inspiring! A friend of mine did a fabulous Raku piece based on her kitchen floor pattern!

Do you have handmade quilts around? Look at the patterns. You can reproduce that effect with carved pieces. I researched Amish quilts for a Smithsonian show. The Amish design that I liked was based on nine squares—does it get any easier than that? I cut several squares so that I could use one stamp for each fabric paint color and not have to clean off the stamps before changing from one paint to another. I stamped onto little fabric squares, and the cards were a big hit.

Go to a fabric store. If a piece of fabric speaks to you, have just enough cut to capture the element you want to carve. I like to carve images from fabric inspirations and then use the fabric and stamp together in one piece of artwork.

Look around your house and studio with a new set of eyes. I pulled apart a doughnut cutter to get two circles. I took the smaller inside circle, pressed it into a piece of carving block and twisted and twisted until the marking was good for going in with my craft knife and cutting it free. That circle has been used as a sun stamp countless times. It is one of my favorite stamps—inspired by a doughnut hole! Go figure. Your junk drawers, too, are full of many design elements staring at you!

I have carved many stamps based on decorative papers. Japanese papers lend themselves to this beautifully. The waves, flowers, symbols, borders— so much packed into each sheet. The fact that many of these papers are printed by hand adds to the feeling of connection. Once again, look for parts within the whole. Innovate and carve.

RUBBER STAMPS AND STENCILS

As rubber stampers, we have probably all said at one time or another, "I love this stamp, but I just wish it were bigger." Guess what? You can carve it, but I will give a cautionary note about copyright infringement—be careful, think and communicate. A stamp company that I loved for years, OM Studio, no longer exists. When I was learning to carve, I enlarged images of some of OM Studio's Tibetan rubber stamps I had purchased and loved working with them. I combined the smaller stamp versions with my larger versions. When making a project for this book using those carved stamps, I literally hunted down the artist, Kel Toomb, who had made the originals, and asked for his permission to show the images in my book. I appreciated his blessing. Using carved images for personal use is one thing, and using carved images for things you will sell is another. Herein lies a good argument for creating your own designs, right?

The very nature of most stencils is simplicity. (I am not referring to the complex brass embossing stencils.) A stencil breaks down an image into components that are separate and cohesive at the same time. You can easily connect those elements for carving if you want to. Chinese characters as stencils or foam stamps are very easy to carve. I highly recommend the book *Stencil It!* by Sandra Buckingham.

Woodblocks from India, Nepal and Tibet have always fascinated me. I have carved my own stamps to simulate some in my collection and to create entirely new blocks with my own signature look to them. You can carve frames to become borders for your blocks or commercial stamps, giving them a whole new look.

PHOTOGRAPHS

Photographs—portraits or scenery or whatever—are a wealth of image inspiration. Some carvers specialize in portrait carving. Personally, I am just learning. Collect photographs— your own, vintage ones, photos from endless sources—and look especially for the ones with strong contrast between light and dark. You can get the high-contrast effect you want by photocopying or by using some computer programs. When the light and dark tones are clear, carving the details is much easier.

9

CARVING ALPHABETS

If I see a word or type of lettering that I like, I cut out examples or make copies of the examples. The number of free fonts available on the Internet is incredible. I liked a font called Playbill. I printed it out and enlarged it on a photocopier. I then carved the alphabet set along with several symbols. (I'll get the numbers done too, someday!)

Staedtler makes a set of small carving blocks as a class pack (there are twenty-seven 1½" [4cm] blocks in the box—perfect for a complete alphabet and one question mark or ampersand). I have always wanted to create my own unique hand-drawn alphabet, so I worked with the size of the blocks, drew out the squares and challenged myself to make letters that fit in the squares as closely as possible.

You can carve several whole-alphabet sets if you like doing that. Some carvers have literally dozens of complete sets. You can also combine commercial alphabet sets with your hand-carved letters. Sometimes you might want to carve just one or two new let-ters. I did an *M* and an *O*, just to be able to write MOM for Mother's Day cards. (Those two letters do get used at other times, too.)

Shadow stamps for your alphabet letters are fun to carve and add a punch of color without having to carve more than a single shadow shape.

With a cardboard alphabet stencil set (get different sizes), you can stencil the letters onto carving material and create a carved stencil set. Use the actual stencils, too, in your artwork to complement the carved images. (Remember to place the stencil facedown before tracing onto the block. It must be reversed in order to print correctly!)

At office supply, art and even toy stores, look for letters that you can translate into carved sets. Mix them up! Some letters are easier to do in certain formats than others. For example, *A, H, I, M, O, T, U, V, W, X* and *Y* are more or less symmetrical. For drawing simple styles directly on the blocks, these are among my favorite characters.

GOING FOR A WALK

Go for a walk and look for architectural elements that you may have walked past a thousand times and never before noticed. I take a little notebook with me for such discovery moments. Old downtown districts, museums, courthouses—all kinds of buildings, with so many details, are there for the looking. I also like to take a camera for some walks, especially in a place like Santa Fe, New Mexico. I have photos of doors and windows that I want to translate into carvings.

Even in a grocery store you can find interesting products with bold graphics to get your creative wheels turning.

Walk into a museum and sketch away. At the Museum of International Folk Art on Museum Hill in Santa Fe, I made several sketches from examples of African Adinkra cloth and used my primitive drawings to understand how to use stamps I had already carved.

When we were kids we used to have picnics in old cemeteries, quiet places with interesting artwork and stories. Some artists render headstone images into beautiful pieces of artwork. Work with photos or actual rubbings to get your images to carve. I would research rubbing techniques first for the correct tools and approach. Care and respect always . . .

EYES OPEN

Keep your eyes open, have a pen and notebook handy, and be ready to enjoy an adventure as you hunt for your image inspirations. They really are everywhere.

CARVING PASSPORT

SPEAKING OF WALKING, LETTERBOXING IS A GREAT ACTIVITY FOR CARVERS! LETTERBOXING IS AN ART NETWORK OF CREATIVE EXPLORERS WHO MAKE ADVENTURES BY LEAVING CLUES AND GATHERING STAMPED IMAGES IN A KIND OF PASSPORT TO SHOW THAT THEY WERE INDEED "THERE." TO LEARN MORE ABOUT THIS TRAVELERS' EXPERIENCE, GO TO WWW.LETTERBOXING.ORG AND SEE WHAT HAPPENS.

MATERIALS FOR CREATING HAND-CARVED STAMPS

Whenever we start a new art form, or expand on an existing one, the exciting though sometimes daunting task of "gathering the tools and supplies" begins. Don't worry: The tools and materials required for carving and printing soft blocks are minimal. Following are descriptions of what's available, but by no means should you assume you will need all of these tools. Read the descriptions, and then shop for what sounds best for you.

CARVING BLOCKS

Soft Blocks

Hand-carving stamps can also be called *eraser* carving, so you might assume that you can just buy erasers and carve them—true enough! However, not all erasers work as well as others, but experimenting does bring some cool findings. For an instant eraser stamp, take your no. 2 pencil and tap the eraser in ink—you now have an instant dot to stamp! Over the years, many new products for carving have come onto the market, and more will surely follow. These soft blocks are a much less intimidating alternative to linoleum. I am going to share with you the five types of soft carving blocks that I work with and why I like them.

PZ Kut by Stampeaz is a nice, stiff, rather thin block. It holds details extremely well. At this time it comes in only one size and two styles: 4¾" x 10" (12cm x 25cm) in a "Premium" grade and a "B" grade. The Premium grade has a very smooth surface on one side and a slightly grainy one on the other. The "B" grade is grainy on both sides with tiny flaws that you can work around. Grainy can be good for certain types of carving to give a little texture.

Mastercarve Artist Carving Blocks by Staedtler are the Rolls-Royce blocks according to some carvers. They are thicker, hold a

great line, usually pricier, and come in various sizes, up to 9" x 12" (23cm x 30cm). The range of sizes is helpful, and the class packs of small square stamps are fun to use. (The Mars white plastic erasers can also be used extensively. These erasers are different than the Mastercarve blocks. They may have an embossed surface detail that must be sanded off.)

Speedy Stamp Carving Blocks by Speedball are pink. They come in several sizes up to 6" x 12" (15cm x 30cm) and also are sold in a beginner's kit that includes a few tools and instructions. The block sheets which are smooth on both sides, are among the most readily available. Most craft and stamp stores carry them along with the Speedball tools.

Soft-Kut Printing Blocks by Dick Blick arrive with powder on the surface, which is easily washed off with water. Soft-Kut is the most pliable of the five blocks and is a bit mushy or rubbery, but I like it a lot. If you need to carve an image that will be stamped onto something rounded, this block is great, because you can wrap it around a surface. A good variety of sizes are available, up to 12" x 18" (30cm x 46cm).

Safety-Kut blocks by Nasco are a great value, and the range of sizes is inspiring. The "Monster Sheet" is 26" x 30" (66cm x 76cm)! One goal I have is to carve a Monster sheet as one stamp

and then print it as a poster-sized print. Nasco also makes a Safety-Kut block with a wood grain texture on the surface.

All of the larger sheets can easily be cut into smaller pieces, of course, and sometimes that is the most economical practice. Do your comparison shopping and see what works.

Many manufacturers advertise that you can carve on both sides of the block—you can. I have done it a couple of times but prefer not to. I tend to carve pretty deep and that can make the blocks weak. Carving both sides does save money, however, so consider it, depending on the type of carving you are doing.

Linoleum Blocks

I never worked with linoleum blocks in school, but I have heard countless stories of people who did, and some of those stories are scary (cut hands and fingers)! Linoleum is difficult to carve, but when you have the technique down, the results are great. For me, linoleum carving is more *printmaking* than stamping, and I look forward to attending college-level classes in the future. An "easy-to-cut" linoleum is now available in some craft catalogs.

Wood Blocks

Relief carving (for printmaking) on wood is the process of carving a flat piece of wood and using it as a printing plate. The most commonly used wood for this type of carving is basswood. The grain allows for detail without splintering. The look of wood-block carving is unique. I have carved wood and then, after printing from it, made copies of the print so that I could translate it into soft block with a different interpretation. Using a wood-grained soft block imitates the look.

Other Surfaces

Many creative printmaking materials are available. Here are a few ideas for you:

Vinyl and plastic erasers from art supply stores and catalogs are great for small projects. Even cheap ones from the dollar stores are workable. They are generally white vinyl, but it is fun to work with other colors, too.

Wine bottle corks have a rough surface, which gives an interesting texture. Use with inks and paints. A friend of mine carves corks and also just stamps with the cork itself—instant polka dots!

Gourds can make great printing blocks. I used a Dremel tool to carve my gourd stamps. These stamps have the look of handmade African calabash stamps, which are used for printing fabrics.

Rubber gasket material can be used for carving. You can buy sheets in different thicknesses at hardware and auto parts stores. Rubber inner tube pieces can also be used. I have cut pieces to make stamps and will try carving them someday. Because of its thinness, this material is easiest to use if it's mounted onto a block.

Flexible printing plate is a very thin carving material with an adhesive back. Cuts need to be shallow, but stamps made from this material print well, especially on paper. Mount these on wood or acrylic blocks, or mount strips onto a rolling pin for a large rolling stamp—very cool. Ink it up on a printing plate or use a foam roller or brush to apply paint or inks on it. Long rainbow inkpads work great too. This material is usually sold in packages of twelve sheets, but some catalogs sell the sheets individually.

Print foam sheets (with or without adhesive backs) are usually available in a package of twelve sheets. These are not meant to be carved into with blades, but they are fun to work with, and children can enjoy them because you don't need sharp blades. Cut out shapes with scissors, or tear them, then mount them onto wood or acrylic blocks.

Inky Rollers (also known as Rainbow Rollers) by Ranger are soft rubber, interchangeable rollers that you can carve. They come in three sizes. Make a variety of your own carved roller stamps. Ink one up and roll!

MagicStamp (also known as PenScore, by Clearsnap) is a great companion to hand-carved stamps. It is a foam that is available either as blocks or as sheets. I use the sheets and mount different sizes on wood blocks. You heat the surface with a heat gun and then press the foam onto the surface of a hand-carved block or other textured objects. This process creates a positive/negative design look when paired with the original stamp. To reuse and create a new MagicStamp image, simply reheat, and press into other surfaces—magic!

13

INKS AND PAINTS

Are you ready to make a print of your carving? Let's talk a little about what you can use. Inkpads for rubber stamps are the ones I started with and still use today. Try to find the ones with raised pads so that inking large stamps won't be a problem. Dye-based (quicker drying) and pigment (good for embossing) inks each have their place, and if you need archival prints, read the labels.

Ink and paint choices are endless and inspiring. I am listing here the products that I have used for years as well as several new ones that stand out. Be careful with permanent inks and solvent cleaners. They are much harsher on soft blocks than on commercial rubber. Block-printing inks are available in tubes or jars. I would recommend using only the water-soluble variety. I like soft rubber brayers for spreading these inks onto the stamps.

Learn what inks and paints work best on different surfaces. Many are multipurpose, and therefore are a good investment. When working with acrylics, buy what is called *acrylic extender* or *retarder* and mix it in with your paints. It will extend the drying time and make stamp cleaning much easier. Acrylics can also be used on fabrics. I suggest adding what is called *textile medium* or *fabric-painting medium* to the paints to make the painted fabric more supple and washable.

PERSONAL INK AND PAINT LIST

Inkpads
Pigment inkpads

ColorBox (Clearsnap)

ColorBox Paintbox, original and 2 (Clearsnap)

ColorBox MicaMagic (Clearsnap)

VersaCraft (especially for fabric and wood) (Tsukineko)

Brilliance (Tsukineko)

Pearl-Ex Stamp Pad (Jacquard)

Dye inkpads

Vivid! (Clearsnap)

Ancient Page (Clearsnap)

Distress Ink (Ranger)

Solvent inkpad

StazOn (Tsukineko)

Other Inks

block printing ink, water-soluble (Speedball and Dick Blick)

All-Purpose Inks (Tsukineko)

Decor it Inks (Ranger)

Paints and Washes

Lumiere (Jacquard)

Neopaque (Jacquard)

Air-Dry PermEnamel (Delta)

assorted acrylics and mediums (Golden, Delta and other name brands)

Walnut Ink (Tsukineko)

Adirondack Color Wash (Ranger)

MARKERS

You can use water-based markers to both ink up your stamps as well as color in after a print is made. When you use them to ink a stamp, brush on the colors and then remember to "huff" on them with your breath to make sure they are moist enough to leave an impression.

POWDERS

Embossing powders give depth and texture to your stamped images. Sprinkle these powders over an image stamped in pigment ink and gently tap off and save the excess. (I use shallow plastic storage containers with lids.) When you melt the powder with a heat gun, the result is a raised look. The color range is vast, but I seem to use metallics and glitter varieties the most.

Mica powders such as Pearl-Ex by Jacquard are fabulous and easy to work with. I use them especially on polymer clay that has been stamped. The mica powders give a highlighting sheen that makes your work shimmer.

Art chalks also can be used. I use cotton swabs to pick up the chalk and add it to the design backgrounds.

CARVING TOOLS

The tools you need for carving stamps are not complicated. You have a surface that needs to be carved, so you need blades. I use two kinds (plus a craft knife):

Soft-Block Carving

Lino cutters by Speedball come with six different blades, including three with V-shape cutters called liners, two *U*-shape gouges and one knife-type blade. Lino cutter blades are numbered 1–6. The red handles are sold individually. I think you need at least three handles to start with. Changing the blades out of the same handle gets old very quickly! You may discover that you use two cutters almost all the time. It is a matter of style. The blades can be changed easily. Speedball Linozip blades are interesting additions. They work with the same red handles, but they are pull-type cutters rather than push-type like the standard Lino cutters.

Staedtler carving tools come as a three-piece set. The blades are labeled 1V, 2V and 5U, which describes the gouge shape. These tools have handles that are more like a pen or marker shape. The blades are not removable so they must be sharpened instead of replaced.

Sharpening tools are a must if you don't want to keep buying new blades. A sharp tool cuts well; a dull tool doesn't. You can use a traditional sharpening stone, but I would suggest the SlipStrop made by Flexcut Tool Company, Inc. It has a special shape that facilitates getting both sides of V- and U-shape gouges.

A craft knife is essential for carving stamps. You need a sharp point and a blade long enough to cut through your blocks. You use this tool for carving as well. It outlines images cleanly and also helps you to do very detailed work that a gouge can't.

Miscellaneous pointed objects such as a wooden skewer can be used to make marks in soft blocks. For years I have used the pointy end of a cheap kids' compass point to make dots in a carving. Little circles can be made with an old ballpoint pen. Old dental tools are in my toolbox, too. Any sharp, pointy instruments can be useful.

Wood Carving

Traditional wood-carving tools are what you need for carving wood blocks. The better the quality, the easier they are on your hands. I do not use them on soft blocks, but you could try it and see if you like the results.

OTHER TOOLS FOR CARVING

Sandpaper

Sandpaper has several uses in carving. Some carvers use very fine grit sandpaper to lightly sand the surface of their carving blocks before doing the design work. They say that it preps the surface for better ink adhesion. Little imperfections and printed labels can be sanded off, but be careful to make the sanding even or you may create "potholes," and your image will print with these imperfections. Then again, that may be what you want! I like to use rough sandpaper to scuff up the surface and edges of shadow stamps and sometimes other stamps to give them a vintage feel.

Dremel

I like power tools and have several in my studio. I heard that some carvers use Dremel tools for carving, so I got one on sale and gave it a try. My opinion: I just don't like the noise. For me, carving is very peaceful, and I like the "hand" element in hand carving. The Dremel was great for carving gourds, however, and it makes great little holes in soft blocks. If I were to use it more extensively, I would buy a special stand for hanging it because your hand gets very tired from the weight. Try wood-block carving with a Dremel or other power tools.

WHEN ADHERING YOUR HAND-CARVED STAMP TO A WOODEN MOUNT, REMEMBER TO INDEX IT FIRST, (MEANING TO STAMP THE IMAGE ON THE SURFACE OF THE WOOD BLOCK SO YOU CAN IDENTIFY IT). USE A PERMANENT INKPAD, SUCH AS VERSACRAFT BY TSUKINEKO, THAT WON'T BLEED ON THE WOOD. IF YOU DON'T WISH TO INDEX IT, YOU CAN SIMPLY ADD A MARKER DOT TO INDICATE THE TOP OF THE IMAGE.

MOUNTING STAMPS

As stamp lovers, many of you will want your carved creations mounted. If you go all out and create really decorative mounts, they make beautiful art pieces in themselves. I love having a few of them in my studio to use. They make beautiful gifts, too.

You can use wood pieces in interesting shapes, cubes, cut bamboo, wine corks, little candlestick holders, toys, plastic containers, and found objects. Stain or paint them, decorate them with tassels, ribbon, wire, beads, beautiful decoupage papers, yarn, sealing wax, glass, and so on! You can create stamps of distinction beyond function. Wood mounts accept rubber cement as an adhesive very effectively. Brush it on the surface of the

stamp and brush it on the wood that will receive the stamp and let them both dry separately. When you put them together at that point, they will have a strong bond. The reason I like this method is because it isn't so strong that you can't separate them if you want to later.

CLEANING AND CARE OF STAMPS

When you have put a lot of time into carving your stamps, you will want to take good care of them.

To clean the stamps after using inks or paints, have a baby wipe or a damp paper towel on a plate or plastic tray handy. If you want to change ink colors or just get paint off before it dries, you can do that right at your art table. With a soft toothbrush, warm water and a little mild soap, gently clean the stamp. Sometimes I use only my fingers to gently wipe the surface under running water. The key word here is gently. Any harsh rubbing can break off delicate pieces of the stamp. After the stamp is washed, put it face down on paper towels for drying. Do not dry or store stamps in direct sunlight.

For storage, I buy lots of acrylic box frames, take out the cardboard insert, and use them as trays. I tend to like the 8½" x 11" (22cm x 28cm) size because they hold a good amount and stack well in my storage area. You must line the bottoms of these acrylic boxes or any plastic container in which you store your stamps. (I like to use Fun Foam sheets from the crafts store, but paper works too.) If you don't, a strange kind of chemical reaction-type bonding can happen between your stamps and the plastic box, and it becomes very hard to get them apart. Also, do not store stamps on top of each other without separation. The weight and pressure from other stamps can cause indentations that will always show up when you stamp.

UNMOUNTED ADVANTAGE

THERE ARE TWO CONSIDERATIONS TO MAKE FOR THE ARGUMENT TO LEAVE THE MAJORITY OF YOUR STAMPS UNMOUNTED: ONE, CLEANING UNMOUNTED STAMPS IS MUCH EASIER. (SOAK THEM IN WATER WITHOUT FUSSING ABOUT KEEPING THE WOOD DRY.) THIS IS ESPECIALLY HELPFUL WITH STAMPS THAT ARE USED FOR FABRICS FOR WHICH PAINTS ARE OFTEN USED. TWO, UNMOUNTED STAMPS SAVE SPACE IN STORAGE UNITS.

The lists below summarize what you will need to begin soft-block printing. The type of carving and printing you get into will guide your needs. Some things you may never need to buy, and some of the things I don't use may appeal to you. If you look in catalogs, either paper or online, go to the printmaking or block printing sections and take it from there.

BASIC CARVING SUPPLY ESSENTIALS

6 Speedball handles, gouges and blades

3 Mastercarve gouges

craft knife and blades

soft-block carving material

self-healing mat

tracing paper (or vellum)

scrap paper

removable tape and/or drafting tape

no. 2 (or softer) pencil

ballpoint pen

permanent marker (fine-line)

metal ruler

acetone (finger nail polish remover)

cotton balls

image to be carved (drawing, tracing, photocopy, etc.)

inks and/or assorted inkpads

baby wipes (alcohol-free) or wet paper towels

soft toothbrush (for cleaning stamps)

SlipStrop sharpening tool by Flexcut (optional)

sandpaper—fine grit to smooth imperfections, rough grit to add surface texture (optional)

good lighting

ADDITIONAL SUPPLIES

Dremel tool with engraving bits

wood-carving tools

assorted needles or pointy instruments

Speedball hand press

baren (for evenly applying pressure)

bone folder

brayers

wooden spoon

multiblock registration board (mine is handmade)

magnifying glass (on stand or with light)

sheet of acrylic or glass (for rolling out ink and for monoprints)

inking plate/bench hook (for inking up and holding a stamp while carving)

heat gun (for embossing)

Rollataq adhesive roller for gluing paper

Uniplast hot glue system for creating sealing wax effects

STAMPING SURFACES— This variety includes the stamps themselves, leaf stencil with texture paint, glazed stoneware tile, fabric, glass and a transparency (over handmade paper).

A picture is worth a thousand words, so I decided to show a few of the surfaces I have worked on using two of my hand-carved stamps.

17

TECHNIQUES FOR STAMPING

In the classes I have taught over the years, my basic philosophy is pretty simple: I will teach you what I know, and I will do it one step at a time. I want you to be comfortable with the tools, and I want you to find your way of working with them. I will show you the way I do it as a beginning point, and then you can find your own style.

There are many different approaches to carving and printing soft blocks. I am not going to try to tell you *everything* about what *everybody* does—I don't even know that myself!

With a few tools, a work surface and a desire to indulge in creative expression, you're ready to begin, but remember a key point about learning to carve: Take your time, be patient with the process and enjoy the results. I am a basic stamper and a basic carver. I like simple (though I also appreciate and stand in awe of complex designs). Some people I know decided to start with carving portraits—wow! I started with an easy fence. I remember being told that if I wanted to teach myself how to play the guitar, I should go for a song that I really wanted to learn and struggle through it. If you love it, you will be willing to spend a lot of time with it.

You can work your way into more complicated carving by taking one step at a time. After you understand and practice the simple methods shown here, you can crank it up! Just try to encourage yourself or imagine that I'm sitting next to you, cheering you on!

PREPARE YOUR SURFACE FOR YOUR IMAGE

Clean your block with mild soap and water. If you want to use a side that has printing on it, like a SKU, you can remove it with acetone (nail polish remover) and a paper towel or sand it off with a fine-grit sandpaper.

SIMPLE BLOCK SHAPES

Sometimes, the shape of the block alone can be just the inspiration you need to get started. I know people who have spent a small fortune on their collection of store-bought shadow stamps and tag stamps, but it is so easy and very inexpensive to create your own. With just a few quick cuts (and scrapes), you're ready to stamp.

A BASIC SHAPE

The most obvious and most versatile shape is the square. Cut out a square from a larger sheet of soft block. You have just created a stamp—congratulations! You can use this shape to stamp with just as it is, or you can alter it further.

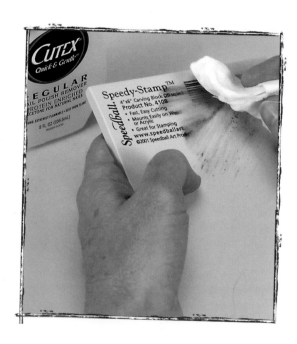

Creating Your Own Shadow Stamp

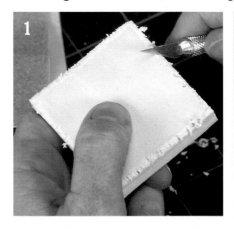

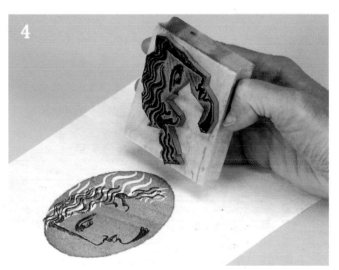

1 CREATE A SHADOW STAMP

Look how easy it is to create your own shadow stamp: Simply cut out a basic shape, like this square, and scrape the edges with a craft knife. Add some scratches in the top surface, and then sand all over the top with rough sandpaper (optional).

2 TRY OUT YOUR STAMP

Here is what this shadow stamp looks like stamped. You can make these easy stamps in any shape or size. You can also rough up the surface of the stamp with a pin or any other sharp tool. Scrubbing it with acetone also changes the surface texture.

3 CONSIDER CARVING AN IMAGE ON THE SURFACE

Shadow stamps can have shapes or other images cut out of their surfaces as well.

4 CREATE A CUSTOM SHADOW STAMP

I created this oval shadow stamp to work as a background for a commercial art stamp. Pair the custom shadow stamp with its complementary image. See how the two images work together? (Art Stamp by Nancy De Santis)

WHEN YOU HAVE AN IMAGE TO CARVE ON YOUR BLOCK, YOU ARE USUALLY GOING TO CARVE AWAY THE WHITE SPACE AROUND THME IMAGE; THE IMAGE TO BE PRINTED IS BLACK (OR BLUE BALLPOINT PEN, OR GRAPHITE PENCIL). THERE ARE ALWAYS EXCEPTIONS, HOWEVER, SUCH AS WHEN YOU MAY WANT TO "DOODLE" WITH THE CARVING KNIFE. JUST MAKE SURE YOU DECIDE CLEARLY BEFORE PICKING UP THE BLADE! CARVE OUT EITHER THE BLACK DRAWING OR THE WHITE SPACE AROUND IT.

Creating Your Own Tag Stamp

A tag is another shape that is so easy to make. You can use your tag stamp as a template over decorative papers, ink it up for colorful background effects, or carve an image into it for your own collage art stamp! The same techniques for edging the shadow stamps can be used on tags as well.

1 CREATE A TAG STAMP ☞

Cut out a square or rectangle block, and then simply cut off two corners. It's easy to round off the corners if you like that look.

2 CUT OUT THE HOLE ☞

To make the hole for the tag, insert your craft blade into the block, hold it at an angle, and then, keeping the knife still, rotate the block in a circle. The blade needs to be very sharp to create a clean hole. When it releases, it looks like a little cone.

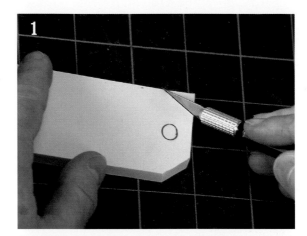

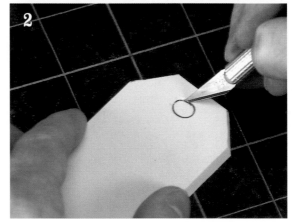

TAGS—By carving your own tag stamps, you have the freedom to go any size or shape, so have fun! The hole reinforcers can be an art in themselves. Stamp on commercial tags, use hardware washers (or cut your own out of interesting paper), then go wild with fibers.

Creating Your Own Faux Postage Stamp

Imagine being freed from the constraints of store-bought templates! When you create your own faux-postage-stamp border, you can have any size or shape stamp your heart desires. You can carve the inside image as well, or you can add art elements, such as actual postage stamps, transparencies, photos, magazine cutouts or even dimensional elements in collage and book arts.

1 CREATE A FAUX POSTAGE STAMP 👉

Did you ever think you'd be able to make your own faux postage stamp? Cut out a shape, and then, using a small U-shape gouge blade, create the perforated border by inserting the blade and pushing out.

2 CUT OUT THE CENTER 👉

You can then cut out a rectangle from the center, so that when you stamp with the faux postage, you have a blank area in which to create an image. Look, now you can use the fall-out for a new stamp!

FAUX POSTAGE STAMPS—What is the correct term? Faux Postage, Postoids, Artistamps . . . There are nuances, it seems, but in general, you can do your own thing with naming! I like to say Artistamps, but we are all talking about postage that is not going to carry the mail. Use these stamps on envelopes as well as in art journals. Whether created in large perforated sheets or made one by one, there is power in having your own postal service!

21

GETTING YOUR IMAGE ONTO THE BLOCK

There are a number of ways to get your image onto your carving block. Four methods are described here to help you transfer your image onto your carving surface. For the methods that use pencil, your design should be retraced onto your block in pen or permanent marker to resist smudging and losing the design while you are handling the block and carving.

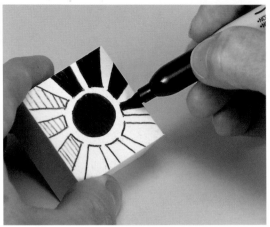

DRAWING DIRECTLY

The simplest way to transfer your image is to draw it directly on the block. Color in the areas that you want to be printed. (You do not have to color in the whole image with marker—just make sure you are clear as to what you want carved away.) Keep in mind that your stamped image will be printed in reverse of how you are drawing it on the stamp. Words are tricky!

TRANSFERRING FROM TRACING PAPER

If you want to draw your design on paper first, you can draw it on tracing paper in pencil. Then, put the image facedown on the stamp and secure it with removable tape. Rub your fingers over the back of the image to transfer the design to the stamp. The image will be light, so you may want to go over it lightly with a pen or marker.

TRANSFERRING FROM REGULAR PAPER

You can also draw on a regular piece of paper with a soft lead pencil and then press the block down onto the paper to transfer it to the block. Press hard. Placing the paper on top works fine, too; remember to press hard with your fingers.

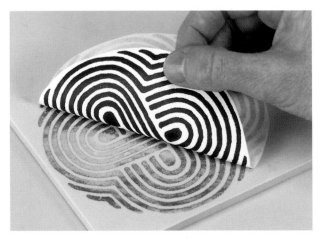

TRANSFERRING WITH ACETONE

For an acetone transfer, start with a fresh laser (carbon-based) photocopy (not an ink-jet). Put the copy facedown on the block, and saturate the back of it with acetone on a cotton ball. Press down with the cotton ball. After you have gone over the entire image, pull the paper off carefully, starting with one corner. If the image is not clear enough, roll the paper back down, soak it with more acetone, press firmly, and lift the image again.

CARVING DESIGNS AND IMAGES

Now that you have an image on your block, you are ready to begin carving it out. Let the tool do the carving. Think smooth and fluid. You want to make as continuous a line as possible. If your design calls for many tiny cuts, that's fine. Just know that the more you start and stop, the more ragged a line can appear. When at all possible, move and turn the block instead of the knife. You will get the feel for this method as you do it. Practice first on a piece of soft block to see what the different blades do. Is there a certain way to hold the handles? Yes—whatever way is comfortable in your hand is the *right* way.

1 REDUCE THE SIZE OF YOUR BLOCK 👉

Choose an image you want to carve, and transfer it onto the block by drawing or using either the acetone or the tracing paper method. Trim away the excess carving material from outside of the image. Either cut straight down or angle your blade to create a pyramid shape. This creates a stable base.

2 TURN THE BLOCK TO CURVE 👉

This design (which I chose from a Dover copyright-free book) is an excellent way to get the feel for carving. Insert your no. 1 v-gouge at the beginning of a line and push with it until you reach the beginning of a curve. Then, holding the blade steady, turn the block in the direction you need to complete the curve. If you wish to include the small circles in the design, cut those out next by just barely inserting your craft knife and rotating the block, while still holding the blade steady.

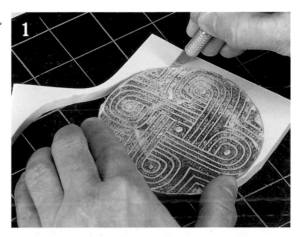

CLEAN UP THE IMAGE

YOU CAN TRY A TEST PRINT WHILE YOU ARE IN THE PROCESS OF CARVING. IT GIVES YOU A FEELING OF WHERE YOU ARE AND WHAT YOU NEED TO DO. I RECOMMEND USING A LIGHT-COLORED INKPAD SO THAT YOU CAN STILL SEE YOUR TRANSFER. CIRCLE THE PARTS ON THE PAPER PRINT THAT YOU STILL WANT TO REMOVE, AND THEN GO BACK TO THE STAMP AND CARVE THOSE SPOTS OUT. WITH THIS LETTER *a* STAMP, I HAD JUST A BIT MORE MATERIAL TO REMOVE FROM INSIDE THE OPENING. TAKE YOUR TIME CARVING MORE AWAY. ONCE IT IS CARVED OUT—OOPS!—YOU CAN'T PUT IT BACK.

Experiment With a Variety of Blades

Chances are, after you have tried several sizes and types of blades, you will return again and again to one in particular. It's good to have a variety on hand, however. Some, like scoop blades, are good for removing a lot of material quickly, but they don't work well for details. Others, like a no. 1 blade, will make detail work a cinch, but you wouldn't want to spend eons removing a large surface area with it. I usually work with about six blades handy. See what works best for you.

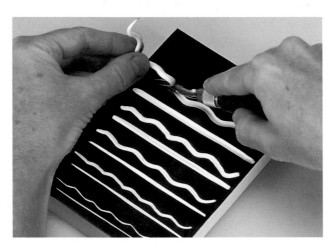

VARY LINE WIDTH WITH PRESSURE

Carving blades come in several sizes and shapes, and each one has a unique purpose. You can vary the width of your line by adjusting how deep you push in the blade. Use all the blades to their maximum advantage.

TRY ALTERNATIVE CARVING TOOLS

There are lots of alternative tools you can use to carve stamps. Here I am using a Dremel tool to create little holes that would be a challenge to carve with blades.

SAFETY FIRST

WHEN YOU ARE USING ANY TOOLS, BE IT A BLADE OR POWER TOOL, USE COMMON SENSE AND TAKE PRECAUTIONS.
* CARVE AWAY FROM YOUR BODY.
* KEEP YOUR HANDS AND FINGERS OUT OF THE LINE OF CUTTING.
* WEAR SAFETY GLASSES WHEN APPROPRIATE.

SPEEDBALL LINO CUTTER

No. 1V   No. 2V   No. 3V   No. 4U   No. 5U

STAEDTLER CARVING SET

No. 1V   No. 2V   No. 5U

SOMETIMES A SIMPLE DRAWING MAKES THINGS THE MOST CLEAR. SHOWN ABOVE ARE THE AVAILABLE SHAPES OF THE SPEEDBALL AND STAEDTLER BLADES.

Experiment Carving Into a Variety of Printing Blocks

Different surfaces deliver different results. Sometimes it's fun to have the texture of the surface itself come through on a print. For the majority of projects in this book I have used stamps carved from soft blocks, but if you can carve into a material with a tool, chances are you can stamp with it. Don't be afraid to try unconventional surfaces. How about car tires, rubber gasket material, cork, all kinds of erasers, and brayers made specifically for carving? Why not carve right into a wooden rolling pin? Imagination wins the day.

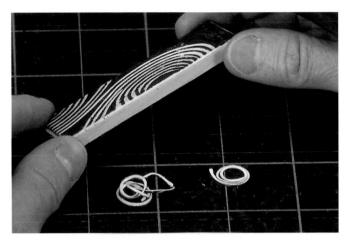

ADHESIVE-BACKED SOFT BLOCK

This ultra-thin adhesive-backed soft block product is designed to be easily cut with scissors, and you can carve into it as well. This one is mounted on a thin piece of pre-cut wood. (I once used a wood rolling pin as a mount.) You may want to consider using a foam cushion between the soft block and the wood, inasmuch as this is very thin material.

ADHESIVE-BACKED FOAM

You can create your own printing plates with this system of adhesive-backed foam, a pair of scissors and a base, such as a piece of wood, heavy cardboard, foam core or mat board, for mounting. This is not created as a carving surface, but you can make indentations with a ballpoint pen to achieve an easy printmaking surface. If you cut out words, remember to do the letters in reverse.

WOOD

Wood-carving tools not only work on soft blocks but on wood, too! (Imagine that.) To achieve a traditional woodcut look on your soft blocks, use soft blocks that have an embossed wood grain or simply leave more lines in your carving to give it a more distinctive handmade look.

GOURD

Here, I used the Dremel tool to carve the surface of a gourd stamp. African Adinkra stamps are hand-carved on calabash (gourd) pieces and then stamped on beautiful, intricately-patterned, symbolic fabrics.

PRINTING WITH YOUR CARVED BLOCK

All of the time spent gathering design inspirations, getting your image onto a block, carving it and looking at your finished stamp leads to one event—printing it! Let's look into the basics of printing and explore some of the supplies we have listed in the materials section. It's playtime!

Using an Inkpad With Your Block

Raised inkpads are the easiest to work with because you are not constrained by the small size of the pad. You can easily ink up even very large stamps. Look for those that say *pigment* or *dye-based* as well as fabric inks and specialty pads. The color variations are endless, from single colors to rainbows.

TAP THE PAD ONTO THE STAMP

The quickest way to ink up a stamp is with a raised inkpad. With the stamp on the table, tap the pad evenly over the stamp. You can also ink up the other way around: Place the inkpad on the table, and then tap the stamp onto it. The size of the stamp and practice will help you determine which method to use.

Using Paint With Your Block

Acrylic paints, latex and fabric paints are easy to use with your carved blocks. Be careful not to apply too much paint so your image will not be garbled. It's important to wash your block immediately after using paint because it is very difficult to remove after it has dried. Consider using paint retarder or extender to avoid drying problems.

DAB PAINT ONTO THE STAMP

You can apply paint to a stamp with a foam brush. Dip the brush into the paint and then tap off the excess onto scrap paper to even out the amount on the brush. Apply paint to the stamp with a dabbing or tapping motion.

TAP, TAP, TAP

TAPPING IS A VERY IMPORTANT CONCEPT. DO NOT PUSH AND TWIST THE STAMP INTO THE INK. IF INK GETS INTO THE CREVICES, IT CAN MAKE A MESSY PRINT.

Using Bleach as a Printing Medium

When we talk about surface design and creating background papers, we are usually referring to adding color or texture to a surface. By using bleach as a printing medium, we are actually removing color to get a very cool effect called *bleach discharge*. I have used bleach on paper as well as on fabric. It is a great look standing alone, but you can also add layers and come in with more color or stamped imagery.

PREPARE A BLEACH STAMPING PAD

Create your own disposable bleach stamp pad by folding paper towels (or white polyester felt) and putting them on a plastic meat tray or ceramic or glass plate. Soak the paper towel pad with standard household bleach. Best results come when the bleach is relatively new. Laundry bleach pens are also fun tools for added effects like handwriting words and making doodle embellishments to complement your carved blocks.

DIFFERENT SURFACES, DIFFERENT RESULTS

The fascinating part is watching what the bleach does! Not every red paper or black paper is going to look the same. The range of results is amazing. I bought three yards of navy blue cotton fabric from different stores to do an art project. I ripped strips from each and then bleached them. The resulting color variations were very interesting, and the amount of bleeding was different in each.

I found that on fabric the bleach bleeds too much and makes the image a little too fuzzy. If I iron it (with a craft-dedicated iron) soon after I stamp, it sets the design more quickly. A very effective product used by fabric artists is called Bleach-Stop, which is made of crystals that dissove in warm water.

Using a Handpress

Some larger stamps are hard to maneuver and ink evenly. A handpress (such as the one offered by Speedball) is a wonderful tool to have, and it isn't very expensive. It works well with stamps that are up to 6" x 8" (15cm x 20cm). I like using my smaller stamps on the press sometimes, too, because it provides a helping hand when you have a lot of stamping to do and you want it done evenly. There are two ways to stamp on a handpress: one, with the paper down and the stamp placed on top of the paper, and two, with the stamp placed faceup and then the paper to be printed placed on top. Both ways work well; it is a matter of experimentation and personal choice.

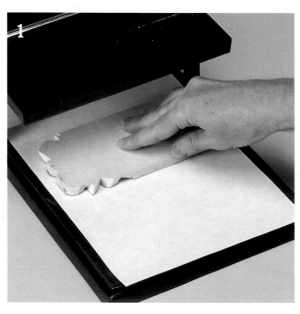

1 SET THE BLOCK ON THE SURFACE OF THE PRESS

Ink up the stamp and set it facedown onto the paper below the pressing plate.

2 PULL THE LEVER

Pull the lever down, and use even, steady, strong pressure to make the print.

3 LIFT THE STAMP OFF

Remove the stamp from the press, peel the paper away if it sticks, and view your print.

Using a MagicStamp

This product is a lot of fun to use! Some artists may know it as PenScore. A representative from Clearsnap told me the creative story behind this very simple art tool. The owner and product designer of the company noticed that the foam-block toys his (then) young daughter loved playing with in the bath had her teeth marks embedded in them—it was one of those genius "aha!" moments that launched a whole new product line. MagicStamp comes in thin blue sheets, which I have mounted on wood blocks. It also comes in various colors as blocks and shapes.

MagicStamp allows you to create images that are a negative impression of your carved blocks. When you add anything that has texture to it as an additional element, your creative possibilities are endless. Words and letters pressed into MagicStamp will reverse themselves and end up backwards when printed, so I stick with images that are more general.

JUNK DRAWER AND MORE

THE ITEMS YOU CAN USE TO CREATE TEXTURE IN YOUR OWN MAGICSTAMPS ARE ENDLESS. FROM NUTS, BOLTS AND MARBLES IN YOUR JUNK DRAWER TO ICE CUBE TRAYS, FABRIC SCRAPS OR HOLIDAY DECORATIONS, A WORLD OF TEXTURE AWAITS YOU!

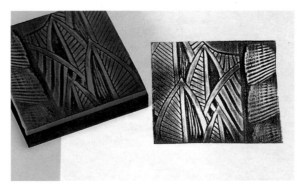

HEAT AND IMPRESS

Heat the surface of this product with a heat gun (for about 30 seconds, continually moving the heat gun to avoid melting the surface). Then impress any image or texture into it. For this stamp, I used a combination of a hand-carved soft block and a sea shell.

TEST THE STAMP

If you are happy with your image, stamp away with it, over and over again! If not, clean the ink off with water, reheat, get your textures onto the surface and stamp again.

29

Using a Brayer and Block-Printing Ink

This method of printing is good for stamps of all sizes, but I especially like it for my largest stamps. Using block-printing ink changes the equation a bit for me. It crosses the bridge from stamping to printmaking. I love the look of the heavy ink that takes many hours to dry. When you use quality Japanese papers or specialty printmaking papers with this method, you really crank it up a few notches (in my humble opinion). There is something about using a brayer that is meditative and relaxing to me. This method is my favorite for printing hand-carved wood blocks. I always use water-soluble block-printing inks on my carved blocks.

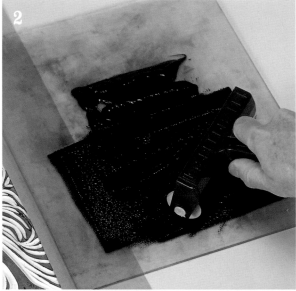

1 SQUEEZE OUT SOME INK

To use block-printing ink, you must first ink up a brayer. It is best to work on a piece of glass or acrylic. Squeeze out a line of ink that is about the same length as the width of the brayer. This makes it easier to roll out and control the spread of the ink. If you are using ink from a jar, use a spatula-type knife or craft stick to lay out a line of ink the length of the brayer's width.

2 ROLL OUT THE INK

Roll out the ink with the brayer, and create a crosshatch motion with the brayer (going up and down, then back and forth). You want the brayer to be coated with a thin, even coat of ink. Globs on the brayer make messy prints, so roll out over and over in a pretty small area to conserve ink.

3 ROLL INK ONTO THE STAMP

Roll the ink onto the stamp with the brayer in an even and all-over motion. Make sure you are covering evenly. I do this with a consistent motion—not fast, but also not letting the inked surface dry before printing. Get more ink off the plate as often as you need to cover the image.

CHEAP ROLLS OF PAPER FROM THE LOCAL PAINT OR HARDWARE STORE CALLED MASKING PAPER, WORK GREAT FOR TESTING PRINTS, ESPECIALLY LONG ONES. MY MASKING PAPERS CAME IN KRAFT AND SAGE COLORS.

4 PRESS THE PAPER WITH A BAREN

Place your paper over the inked image, smooth it down gently and evenly with your hand, and then apply pressure over the image with the baren. This is called *burnishing*, and it can also be done with the back of a wooden spoon or your hand. Circular and linear motions work well. Be careful not to push the paper in a sliding way (it will blur the print). Rub with even pressure over the entire surface.

5 PULL THE PRINT

Beginning at one end, gently pull the paper off of the stamp. This is known as "pulling the print."

6 WASTE NOT, WANT NOT

Wait! Don't rinse off that inking plate just yet! Let's turn it into a *printing* plate. You can make a very cool monoprint with the ink that is left. Spread out the ink some more, if you like, then squeeze a new color of ink or paint (any kind, I used acrylic) onto the plate in some kind of design, such as a spiral. Now press stamps randomly into the paint and pull them off.

7 PULL A MONOPRINT

Now lay a piece of paper over the plate and rub with either your hands or a baren, and *voila!* A great monoprint! These papers make excellent background papers for all kinds of art projects. The ink left on the plate is called the ghost—you can try to print from that, too.

MULTIPLE MONOPRINTS

YOU CAN USUALLY GET SEVERAL MONOPRINTS FROM ONE PLATE. I KEEP A SPRITZER WATER BOTTLE HANDY, SPRITZ THE SURFACE, ADD A LITTLE MORE INK OR PAINT, ALTER THE STAMPS AND KEEP GOING UNTIL THE PLATE IS BASICALLY DRY. EVEN VERY LIGHT PRINTS WORK WELL BECAUSE YOU CAN USE THEM AS BASE PAPERS FOR LAYERED STAMPING.

Creating a Multi-Block Print

A multi-block print is created with at least two blocks that are carved and printed one over the other. We can achieve different effects, either aligning images to look like they are parts of a puzzle that fit together, or layering, overlapping and intersecting colors. I am going to use a registration board that I designed and made from simple parts, but you don't need one to begin making multi-block prints. Just make sure that you have marked registration points in a couple of places for clean alignment. Two corners work well for starters.

There are a couple of carving techniques that intimidated me for a long time and so I wasn't drawn to them. Multi-block prints were one of them. I am going to present the most basic method to you here, because that is all I know! Let's learn together . . .

1

TRY THIS!

TRY MAKING A MULTI-BLOCK PRINT USING ONLY ONE BLOCK. START WITH A SQUARE PIECE OF CARVING MATERIAL. CARVE RANDOM GEOMETRIC DESIGNS. WITH THIS ONE BLOCK, TRY STAMPING WITH DIFFERENT COLORS OF INKS, ROTATING THE STAMP EACH TIME, AND CLEANING OFF THE BLOCK BETWEEN INKS. IT WILL BE FUN TO SEE WHAT HAPPENS! THE OVERLAPPING COLORS WILL CREATE NEW COLORS. TRY THIS WITH A ROUND BLOCK, TOO.

1 PREPARE STAMP NUMBER ONE

Start with a sketch done in pencil on white paper. From there, use tracing paper to figure out how you want to break down the designs into color layers. Three major blocks make up this design. Using tracing paper, transfer each desired layer directly onto identically sized blocks. Carve all of the blocks. Pin the printing paper to the top of the board with two pushpins. Ink up the first stamp, and place it snugly into the corner of the frame.

2 PRINT STAMP ONE; PREPARE STAMP TWO

Roll the paper down over the inked stamp, and then use a baren to print it. Lift the paper up and back slowly, and then put a weight on it so you can set up the next stamp. Remove stamp number one and then replace it with stamp number two.

2

BACKGROUND CHECK

32

YOU CAN USE THE BLANK BACK OF ONE OF THE BLOCKS TO DO A SOLID BACKGROUND COLOR LAYER IN THE BEGINNING. EXPERIMENT WITH LIGHT-COLORED INKS AND STAMP THE BASE BLOCK TO BRING IN SUBTLE TEXTURE.

3 INK UP STAMP TWO; PREPARE THREE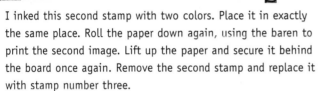

I inked this second stamp with two colors. Place it in exactly the same place. Roll the paper down again, using the baren to print the second image. Lift up the paper and secure it behind the board once again. Remove the second stamp and replace it with stamp number three.

4 PRINT STAMP THREE

I inked up the third stamp in black. Using the same process as before, print with the baren. You now have a three-block multi-print. (I also carved one small piece that is the exact size of the sun. This allowed me to add more color just to that specific area, if I wanted to.)

5 TOUCH UP MISSED AREAS

Remove the paper from the registration board. If you want to, you can touch up any missed areas. Imperfections can also be viewed as a signature that this piece is actually handmade, so take that into consideration. Sometimes I touch up, other times I leave things alone and enjoy the anomalies.

INTERCHANGEABLE BLOCKS

TRY CARVING DIFFERENT COMPONENT PIECES AND LAYING THEM OUT TOGETHER AT ONE TIME TO GET A TOTAL STAMPED IMAGE. YOU CAN EVEN MAKE PARTS THAT ARE INTERCHANGEABLE. THINK OF THIS PROCESS AS A LAYERED PUZZLE!

CARVING A PORTRAIT

Portraits can be very bold and graphic or extremely detailed with the finest lines. From self-portraits to famous folks, from your children to retro cartoons, it is fun to interpret a portrait in a carving.

The key point to carving a portrait is to work with images that have excellent contrast between light and dark areas. I do this by going to the local copy center (late at night) and playing with the images. I take a bunch of photos with me from different sources and generally pick ones that already have some kind of simple line or color contrast. The first copy I make is to lighten the ink tone. This allows a lot of gray tones to drop out completely. Then I size things up or down and print a dark copy. Then, I take that copy and make a copy of that. I keep going, making several generations of that image until I have what I think will work for carving. You can also change the contrast levels using image editing programs on your computer.

FROM PHOTOCOPY TO PRINT—In this sample, I started with an old photograph by Edward S. Curtis. The dark sepia tones brought me a step closer right from the beginning. I reduced the size of the photo, and then worked with the copier until I had the contrast that I wanted. I started working with these images for printing on handmade cards that I created for museum shops in the Southwest.

The key to a portrait is the eyes. Depending on how detailed you want to be, they can be the most difficult. Study the ways the artists handled eyes for their Artist Trading Cards in the Portrait Gallery on page 110 and 111. There are many styles. You can go from a shadow/silhouette style to photorealism.

1 STAMP THE BACKGROUND 👉

I used two stamps for this image, but only the carved one is necessary. The one on the left is the carved portrait stamp itself, and the other was created to easily add background color. When you are creating a background color stamp, make sure that it is in exactly the same position as the carved image so that you are adding color where you want it. I like using a permanent marker so that I have a clear delineation between elements.

2 STAMP THE FIGURE 👉

For this print, I used the background stamp. I just inked up the turquoise section in the corners and then printed the portrait carving in black on top. Be careful to line up the stamps. I find that two corners and one side work well as registration points.

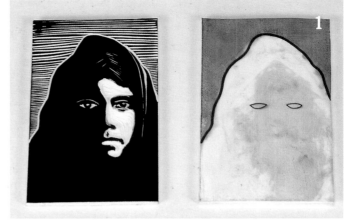

THE OPEN WINDOW—We can do portraits from photos, and we can also do architectural or other types of carvings based on photos or paintings. This stamp design was based on a photo of a painting by artist Andrew Wyeth. I drew a pencil sketch of his painting, transferred my pencil drawing to the carving block and carved from that.

DEVELOPING YOUR ARTISTIC IDENTITY

CREATING YOUR SIGNATURE LOOK

On these next four pages, I would like to share with you on a bit of a different level. By this I mean, there are no "how-to" directions, nor is there a description of a project or a technique. This section is more about an attitude, a way of thinking and a way of life expressed in the art we create—a bit of a philosophy without philosophizing!

When you look at any of your favorite art books or magazines, there is a general character or *feel* to the publication. We gravitate to some more than others. As we flip the pages, we stop and drool over some work and skip right on over others. If we see an artist's name whose work we love on the cover of the magazine, we buy the magazine without even opening it! We just know we want it.

Can we be disappointed? Sure, but the way I look at things, I always learn something new and feel very grateful for the generosity of artists who share by baring their souls and revealing techniques that are oftentimes very personal.

While preparing my proposal for this book, I wanted to bring to the North Light table a group of artists to create "the carving art gallery of my personal dreams" that would elevate this book beyond my own offerings. I made a list of artists whose work has a strong signature look to it and art that I have been drawn to over the years. Many of these artists I have admired from afar and I was nervous about contacting many of them. There is a certain vulnerability there, but I sure wasn't going to pass up the possibility of a few of them agreeing to participate. As I shared my vision for this book with each person, I was so moved by the responses. From master carvers to artists who had never before used carved blocks in their work but wanted to dive in and give it a whirl, *every single person* said yes. I am so grateful for the enthusiasm and support they gave me from the very beginning. The spectrum of artwork is truly inspirational.

Each of these artists has specialties, and each has a forever-expanding range. Therein lies one of the secrets of developing your artistic identity and creating your signature look. Do what you love and express your personality. Don't get stuck there—feel free to go to new venues, which are ultimately your heart and soul. The mediums may change and evolve, like you do. You are not confused, you are creative, and that is a signature look in and of itself.

Years ago, I was in my (then) unfinished basement studio, showing friends where I did my card business when the phone rang; it was the Smithsonian calling! The main buyer for the shops had just been in New Mexico looking for products and kept turning over these handmade cards, shop after shop, from Santa Fe to Albuquerque. The cards were all very different, but all had my name on the back! She was drawn to my *look*. She wanted to know how I achieved my signature look that carried through many different card lines. Now, the Smithsonian wanted a distinctive ImpressionsArt Designs card line of their own. Oh my—a challenge . . .

I listened to what she was considering. I drew some new designs, carved a set of new stamps and sent her prototypes of the cards. I worked very hard on those cards—they were going to the *Smithsonian* after all! The buyer, a professional graphic designer herself, called me and said, "Gloria, these are nice, but something is missing. In trying to do something impressive for us, you forgot who you are and what we like about your work." I was a little taken aback ("stunned" is a good word) and asked what it was that they saw in New Mexico that they didn't see now. It was a certain spontaneity, a kind of boldness and detailing that I missed when I was fussing with their set. I will always remember what she told me: that I needed to just make *my* cards, not cards that I thought they would like. Do it my way. It was, and is, a learning curve that I still explore to this day. I went back to the drawing board, opened a *Somerset Studio* magazine, learned a technique with hot glue sticks that looked like sealing wax, and have made cards for the Smithsonian Renwick Gallery Shop and later, their Dulles International Airport Shop ever since.

Have the card designs changed over the years? Yes, but that sealing-wax look has remained. I can't stand to be bored, so I do make changes. Is there a signature look that says these are my cards? Absolutely, so let's talk about how this happens.

A SPIRAL HAND, A HOLY MACKEREL AND A SUN BY THE MESA: LOGOS, SYMBOLS AND IDENTITY

A Spiral Hand

I wanted to have a symbol that said, "I made this artwork *by hand.*" I wanted it for my personal artwork as well as for the business aspect of my work. I have always had an affinity for the beauty of hands. While in Santa Fe walking along an arroyo, the thought came to me: "Impressions" will be the name of my studio, and my symbol will be a hand with a spiral as the palm. Ancient cave artists signed with their own hands. I would sign with one, too! The spiral meant "journey," and I was on one.

I drew a simple image of my idea, using pencil on paper, then transferred it to a tiny piece of carving material, and there it was. Need a logo? Carve it! I have stamped that original stamp more times than I could ever count. I sign my name right next to it.

Over the years, I have used the hand idea as a base and carved many different hands to expand on that original concept. From brochures to business cards, from flyers announcing shows and classes to personal greeting cards and magazine submissions, invoices, packing slips, and on and on. When you see my work or correspondence, you know it's mine. My work evolves with a fluent motion, connected by distinctive symbols and themes.

A Holy Mackerel

When I was a kid we always said, "Holy moly!" and "Holy mackerel!" I never knew what a moly was, and I didn't realize until much later that a mackerel was a fish. And what is holy about mackerels? Linguists may help us out, but I just liked saying those phrases, no matter what they meant. When I had my own kids I made up the phrase, "Holy moly mackeroly!" and it was a fun part of the family lingo.

Then one day I had this brainstorm to write a memoir-type book about creating my home-based art business. I wanted a wild title, and I wanted to do it all—the way I wanted to do it. I knew that no publisher on earth would ever go along with all of my strange ideas. So, I took the biggest financial (and personal) risk of my life up to that point—I published

it myself. The wild title? *Holy Moly Mackeroly! . . . from 3 Art Stamps to the Smithsonian . . . Reflections on the Business of Art and the Art of Life.*

I needed cover art. What do you do when you need cover art? Carve it! I went to the local grocery store and bought a 99¢ can of mackerel with a good fish graphic on the label. I cut off the label, gave the can of mackerel to my husband, then played around with the image, changed it, and added a smile and a halo ("holy"). With additional carved pieces made to create a frame, I had the cover art—a total of six carved stamps. I asked an art student friend of mine to do the cover layout, and, in time, I became the holymolymama.

A book is one level and one step. It's the ripple effects that have changed my life. To see that fish travel to different parts of the world—to have an online group founded by fans of the book (with the cover as the group logo), to have aprons made for the First Annual Holy Moly Art Retreat in Southern California, and to have them worn by friends of the lifelong variety—what a blast and what an honor.

Take a wild idea and go with it. You might want to question your sanity; you might not. I don't anymore. People may love it, people may hate it, but the point is this: I took a huge chance and have no regrets and many incredible stories that don't seem to stop.

A Sun by the Mesa

When you get all worked up and inspired and think you can do anything, even with no money, well, things seem to get moving around you, ready or not. I was writing for two years and doing my art business at the same time. It got to the point where I needed a publishing company name for the unbelievable amount of paperwork and bureaucratic hoops I had to jump through. I couldn't come up with one. I went through months of scratching off endless dumb names. (The publishing company name couldn't be too weird, I figured.)

At 2:00 in the morning, my husband and I both couldn't sleep and found ourselves in the kitchen. I told him that I needed a publishing company name by the morning (more accurately, later the same morning). He told me that there was a company in the Southwest whose name he really liked. We looked online together, and he showed me "Chamisa Ridge." We went back to the kitchen, and discussed it. Okay, we didn't want to copy it, of course, but we liked the feeling. We threw around a whole bunch of words, like *arroyo* (dry river bed—sounded depressing), *yucca* (laughed), and several Spanish words. Then Gary said, "What about *mesa*?" "Yeah, that's good. Now what about the second word?" We talked about how someday, at some point in our lives, we would like to move to the Southwest, a destination and a destiny—a *point*! Mesa Point. Thank you very much.

I registered the name legally later in the day, and a few days later asked Gary to draw a sketch for me of his idea of a Mesa Point. Based on his sketches, I drew a larger version, and if you need a publishing company symbol, you can—*carve it*!—which I did.

The point of sharing these stories is to prove that it's all so doable for anyone. Now, my collection of carved and commercial stamps includes many hands, fish, waves and suns. Mixing them together is fun and gives me flexibility as I say, "This is me." I have had commercial stamps made, based on my original carvings. I can carve the image large, but sometimes I want very small images (for letterheads and such) and I do not feel I can physically duplicate the design as detailed as I want it. I had my Mesa Point and Holy Mackerel carvings reduced and reproduced and use them on mail art and business correspondence. They have provided a good connection between carving and the beauty of traditional rubber.

PUTTING YOUR HEART AS WELL AS YOUR ART INTO YOUR PRESENTATIONS

A trademark of mine is making the packaging an experience for the person receiving it. Whether it is an envelope or a box with art submissions, a book that is ordered or a bill that I am paying, I pay attention to the way I send things. I like the thought that invoice that I have stamped may make the person opening it smile. My products are not just "things," and I hope that my presentation gets that point across. I know that a fair amount of my artistic effort probably goes unnoticed, but that isn't my part of the statement. (You can easily get carried away with this, so I include a cautionary note here!)

I have heard and seen that people actually keep some of the boxes I have shipped; they just don't want to throw them away! I can't let go of mail art envelopes that I receive. My collection grows, and it is inspiring. I appreciate the art and the *heart*.

Make an impression when you want to. A dear friend of mine told me, "You have only one chance to make a first impression." An impression is a form of giving as well as a form of communicating and advertising. Most of it gets tossed, but the energy invested is never lost. It is invested in who you are and what voice you sing to the universe.

I had fun making my presentation to North Light. I had even more fun when I heard that they liked it! The experience of submitting artwork to magazines and other publications is enhanced when I decorate the box or envelope and hear from the editors and publishers that they loved not only what was sent but the way it was sent. I appreciate their appreciation! Even if the submission isn't accepted, the connection is there for the future. When people look forward to hearing from you, that is a good thing.

Think of who you are and how you would like to express yourself. My art themes tend to be Asian and Southwestern as well as folk art from different cultures. My color schemes tend to be strong and earthy. You may love Victorian and pink! If so, lace things up! Get the vintage look going, and immerse yourself in the atmosphere in which you feel at home. Create from that place and invite others for a visit. I'd love to come over.

Perhaps a feather, a kimono or a willow chair would be a nice symbol for you. Maybe you like tuna fish instead of mackerel, or perhaps a monogram of your initials as a signature would work for you. You can find a design and develop it over time. Nothing in a creative life is static. Your artistic personal and public identity is yours to explore. As artists, we have chosen a wide-open territory for our trek. Connect with it, embrace it, and most important—enjoy it!

REFLECTIONS

A personal creative style isn't manufactured instantly; it evolves, which means it can change. Don't be afraid of that. The essence of your signature look is a way of life, not the things you produce.

The art of presentation adds significantly to the perceived and real value of your artwork. There were times when I spent as much energy on my art show displays as the art itself. When other artists took note of how my husband and I designed and created various display options, we felt complimented and sometimes copied. That was fine; the concepts were very helpful—glad we could help.

Call your art space your studio, even if it is a table and a chair. It all starts somewhere—it might as well be here and now. Gradually expand your space and your mental and physical horizons. If my studio setup is not working the way I like to work, then nothing works! For me, it means that things are organized, accessible and affordable. Some artists need what I perceive to be chaos. For them, creative freedom lies in having stuff everywhere. Know thyself and go from there.

Correspondence, shipping packages—whenever something needs to go from me to another person, I think about the receiver. What am I sending you? Will you smile when this comes to your hands and home? Will your life be enhanced a bit by this? If so, then it is a gift. Forget guilt. If I took the time to personalize everything the way I idealize it in my mind, nothing would ever get out of here. Give yourself a break and at least put a nice postage stamp on the envelope as you dash out to catch the postman.

Life is like a river; it can be churning, white-knuckling whitewater or meandering and calm with lapping water on a peaceful shore. It can be both within minutes of each other. Remember to enjoy the ride. The river is only so long. Row with style, and when necessary, row like crazy!

We live in a high-tech world, and that has its ups and downs. The fact that we are artists and make things by hand brings an earthy, natural element to society. Realize the value of art and craft. Tie history and the future together with your hands and vision.

Shoot high for your ideals and let reality be comfortable at the same time. I like to learn from other artists. Consider being part of an art group of friends who meet regularly. I have done this monthly for many years. Start a group of just two or three people. It's amazing how much your style is sparked when you're around people who express theirs freely.

Participate in art exchanges that push the boundaries of what you think you do well. You'll find out a lot about yourself in the process of making new art. It may be frustrating or scary or exciting, but it isn't boring!

Give yourself "play challenges" from time to time. Example: Make three cards using one carved stamp, each in a color theme that you never work with (and perhaps, don't even like)—go for it!

I tend to grimace at the word *image*. It feels superficial and a bit cosmetic to me. I know of people who seem to be slaves to their image. "What image am I projecting? What image am I protecting?" "Image" can go deeper than that. Your image can simply be what you decide to express and what you give. Then you are never a slave to the expectations or demands of others. Your reflection pleases you, and that is what counts.

STAMPING ONTO PAPER

PAPER IS THE FIRST SURFACE WE USE WHEN STAMPING our hand-carved images. We test them on scrap paper, and that first glimpse is our beginning point. If we are satisfied, we print more. If we need to make adjustments, we carve again until we get the effect we want.

From cardstock to printmaking paper, from lovely, natural handmade Japanese papers to inexpensive copy paper and recycled paper bags, paper is an artist's dream surface. When you carve specifically for paper, you get a two-dimensional print. When you use carved blocks in wet paper pulp, you add another dimension—what you have carved away now becomes a texture rather than open space. You now have embossed handmade paper.

Whichever paper art you prefer, I can say with confidence that carved stamps will become an art tool of choice.

WHAT YOU NEED

white cardstock, 5" x 5"
(13cm x 13cm)

black inkpad {COLORBOX}

acetate or vellum, 5" x 5"
(13cm x 13cm)

tape

pencil

craft knife (or paper cutter)

cutting mat (optional)

Rollataq (Daige) adhesive or glue stick

Japanese paper, 2" x 11"
(5cm x 28cm)

black cardstock, 5½" x 5½"
(14cm x 14cm)

Thai mango paper, red 8½" × 11"
(22cm × 28cm)

ruler

ready-made frame, 8½" × 11"
(22cm × 28cm)

bamboo placemat (optional)

templates for carvings provided on page 122

FRAMED ARTWORK

Framing a piece of your artwork adds a dimension that allows you to display your creations. From a single piece to a grouping, framed art enhances your home and studio décor. Store-bought frames make the project quick; adding an element such as a bamboo placemat as a background makes the piece stand out in a unique way. Create a grouping for impact. This project incorporates carved stamps with simple paper-layering effects.

STAMP CARVINGS

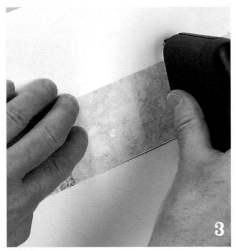

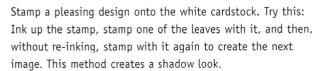

1 STAMP THE ARTWORK

Stamp a pleasing design onto the white cardstock. Try this:
Ink up the stamp, stamp one of the leaves with it, and then,
without re-inking, stamp with it again to create the next
image. This method creates a shadow look.

2 CROP AND TRIM

Use the 5" × 5" (13cm × 13cm) acetate or vellum as a
cropping tool to decide your composition. When you have an
area that you like, tack down the vellum with tape, and use
a pencil to mark where you will need to trim the piece with
a craft knife or paper cutter.

3 APPLY ADHESIVE

Using the Rollataq applicator (or a glue stick), apply adhesive
to the back of the Japanese paper strip.

4 ADHERE THE JAPANESE PAPER

Adhere the Japanese paper strip to the red piece, positioning
it 1¾" (4cm) from the right side.

5 ADHERE THE STAMPED PIECE

Roll adhesive onto the back of the white stamped piece
and glue it to the black cardstock square. Position that piece,
2½" (6cm) down from the top and 2½" (6cm) from the right
side. The piece is now ready to put into the frame.

FINISHING DETAIL

TRY USING BAMBOO PLACEMATS AS BACKGROUNDS FOR FRAMED PIECES.
CREATE A HANGER WITH A THIN-GAUGE WIRE THAT BLENDS WITH THE
BAMBOO. HANG THE PLACEMAT ON THE WALL AND THEN PLACE A NAIL
BETWEEN SLATS TO HANG THE FRAMED PIECE OVER IT.

LUMINARIA

In New Mexico, a friendly "discussion" takes place each holiday season debating whether these traditional lighted paper bags are called *luminarias or farolitos*. Either way, they are a lovely addition to any festive occasion. Create a long line of luminarias leading to your home, creating a welcoming path of light. Use them indoors for a warm glow. For any occasion, for any time of year, give this old tradition a new and personal expression.

44

STAMP CARVINGS

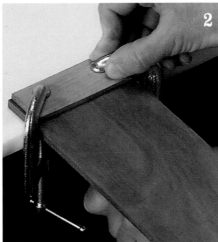

1

2

3

1 FOLD DOWN THE BAG

Fold down the top of the bag twice, about 1" (3cm) each time, so that the total height of the bag is 8½" (22cm). This will keep the shape stiffer and the bag stronger.

2 SET UP A STAMPING SURFACE (OPTIONAL)

To create an easy surface on which to stamp, clamp your hardwood board to the edge of the table. This board creates a surface for the open bag. Cut the wood to accommodate the side panel width.

3 STAMP ONTO THE BAG

Slide the bag over the end of the wood. Tape the bag to the board, if you like. Begin stamping onto the first side of the bag, and then turn the bag to stamp on all sides. If you aren't using the clamps and board, fold the bag to stamp on the front and the back, and forego stamping on the sides.

4 FILL THE BAG

After stamping is complete, let the ink dry. Then, put about 2" (5cm) of sand or tiny pebbles into the bottom of the bag.

5 LIGHT THE CANDLE

Set your candle into the bottom of the bag, and light the candle with a long-necked lighter.

4

BAG IT!

TO CREATE A TEMPLATE FOR OTHER TYPES OF PAPER BAGS, TAKE APART A REGULAR BAG AND TRACE IT ONTO A LARGE PIECE OF HANDMADE OR OTHER TYPE OF PAPER. FOLD ALONG THE SAME LINES TO RE-CREATE THE BAG, AND GLUE THE BAG TOGETHER WITH DOUBLE-STICK TAPE OR GLUE STICK.

DECORATIVE PAPER
LUMINARIA

Take the look of the traditional luminaria and create one with a wooden base, using decorative papers. Your own handmade paper or handmade papers from around the world will take the place of paper bags and will give you many surfaces to experiment with. It's also easy to stamp, since you are beginning with a flat sheet of paper rather than a folded paper bag. Have fun experimenting with the effects of using various colored papers.

WHAT YOU NEED

skeleton leaves handmade paper, 18" × 11½" (46cm × 29cm)

black inkpad (pigment or dye-based)

gold acrylic paint

craft glue

block of wood, 3½" × 5" × ¾" (9cm × 13cm × 19mm)

stapler

votive candle and holder

template for carving provided on page 122

1 WRAP THE PAPER AROUND THE BLOCK

Fold the top portion of the paper down twice lengthwise, 1" (3cm) each turn. Lay your paper out, stamp and paint to get the design you are happy with, then let it dry. Place a line of glue around the edge of the block and along the long, bottom edge of the paper. Wrap the paper around the block.

2 SECURE THE SEAM

Glue the seams of the paper together, and secure the paper to the board with a stapler. Stapling will also help secure the paper while the glue dries.

LUMINARIA
VARIATION

Here is an interesting variation:
Try stamping with linseed oil to get
a glowing effect when you light the
candles inside the paper bags. The
linseed oil tends to really bleed into
the paper, so use very chunky-style
stamps. You can try to control the
bleeding by using a heat gun to dry it
more quickly, but beware of the fumes!
I outlined the linseed oil designs with
a black fine-line marker, which gave
the designs some definition.

GLASS
LUMINARIAS:
FIRE AND WATER

From paper to glass; from sand
to water. This variation starts
with glass vases from the craft
store. Add stones or glass marbles inside the vase, then float
candles in water and decorate
the vase exterior with bands of
stamped paper or fabric, fibers
or ribbon. Change the bands to
suit the occasion. Stamp hot
glue seals for a finishing touch
(see step 7 on page 52).

47

WHAT YOU NEED

cardstock 8½" × 11" (22cm × 28cm), one each:

- brick red
- plum
- black

bone folder (optional)

black inkpad (COLORBOX)

removable tape

gold glitter embossing powder

clear embossing powder

heat gun

red cardstock, 4" (10cm) square

magnetic strip, two 1" (3cm) pieces and two 2" (5cm) pieces

glue stick (or adhesive of your choice)

white paper, 3¾" (10cm) square

decorative paper, ¾" x 5¼" (19mm x 13cm) and 5½" (14cm) square

templates for carvings provided on page 122

MAGNETIC BOOKMARK CARD

This special card is a gift in itself with two bookmarks as part of the card design. Creating a triptych with a square card format is easy and elegant. The papers, carved stamp images and colors are harmonious. With the cutting technique used here, you will have enough pieces to create three separate cards, if you wish. It is a useful gift that doesn't need to end up in a drawer—how about in a book or art magazine instead?

48

STAMP CARVINGS

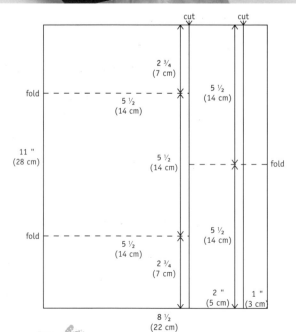

1 TRIM THE CARDSTOCK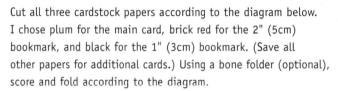

Cut all three cardstock papers according to the diagram below.
I chose plum for the main card, brick red for the 2" (5cm)
bookmark, and black for the 1" (3cm) bookmark. (Save all
other papers for additional cards.) Using a bone folder (optional),
score and fold according to the diagram.

2 STAMP OVER THE CLOSED CARD

With the flaps of the card closed, stamp over the surface of
the front of the card using the wave stamp and the black ink.
Use scrap paper for over-stamping (when the image runs off
the edge). To hold down the flaps, roll pieces of removable
tape and tape down the flaps from the inside of the card.

3 EMBOSS THE IMAGE

Sprinkle gold embossing powder over some of the images and
clear embossing powder over the rest, and then heat with the
heat gun.

4 CREATE THE BOOKMARKS

Stamp the floral and lined images onto the front of the red
bookmark strip. Sprinkle gold embossing powder onto the
flower center and just a bit of the striped areas. Sprinkle clear
embossing powder over the rest of the inked area, then heat
all of the powder to melt it. Use glue stick to adhere the
magnetic strips to the insides of the bookmarks, at the top
and bottom of each.

5 ADD DECORATIVE PAPERS

Glue the small strip of decorative paper to the front of the
black bookmark, and then glue the square of decorative paper
to the inside of the card. Layer the red cardstock square and
then the white paper square onto the center of the card to
finish. Position the bookmarks over the flaps of the cards.

49

WHAT YOU NEED

large craft sticks, three

ochre-colored stain

rag or paper towel

black inkpad {VERSACRAFT}

black corrugated matboard,
7" x 6" (18cm x 15cm), two pieces

⅛" (3mm) hole punch

bone folder

hot glue gun

black hot glue stick

squeeze clamps, two

black wire, 20-gauge, three 10"
(25cm) lengths

round-nosed pliers

assorted beads

torn natural-tone handmade paper
(to layer with papyrus)

craft glue

inking plate

brayer

black block-printing ink (water soluble)

dark brown papyrus paper (cut to fit the cover)

assorted decorative threads and fibers,
5" (13cm) each

metallic copper inkpad {COLORBOX}

acrylic paint, copper and gold {LUMIERE}

sealer of your choice

assorted textured papers for pages,
7" × 6" (18cm × 15cm)

templates for carvings provided on page 122

ARTIST'S JOURNAL

Creating art journals with coordinating bookmarks presents a great opportunity to make unique covers for book arts. These journals can be large or small, and they can have as many internal pages as you would like to include with a variety of textures inside and out. Using large craft sticks for strengthening the book binding and the bookmarks allows you to play with the effects of staining and stamping on wood as well as adding fiber and sealing-wax effects.

STAMP CARVINGS

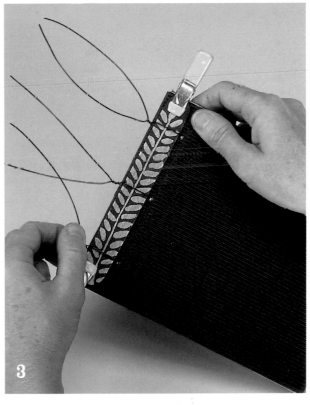

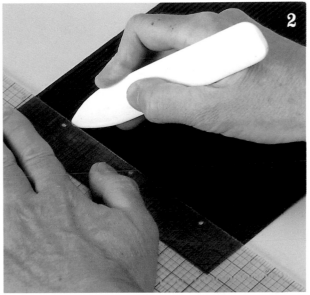

1 STAIN AND STAMP THE CRAFT STICKS 👆

Stain the three craft sticks with the ochre stain, and rub off the excess with a rag or paper towel. Stamp onto the three sticks with the black ink.

2 PUNCH AND SCORE THE COVERS 👆

Along each short end of the two corrugated matboard pieces, punch three ⅛" (3mm) holes, one in the center and the other two, 1" (3cm) in from each end. All three should be 1" (3cm) from the outside edge. Using a bone folder, score a line just to the side of the holes to allow the covers to open easily.

3 SEW THE BOOK TOGETHER 👉

Glue one stamped craft stick to the edge of each cover, front and back. Using one cover as a guide, punch holes through the interior pages at the same three spots. Line up the covers and all of the pages, and clamp the pieces together with a couple of squeeze clamps. Thread a length of wire through each hole, and twist the two ends together about three times.

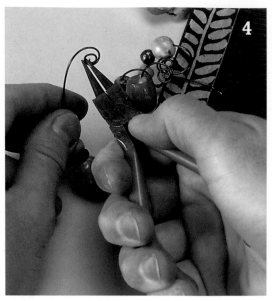

4 ADD BEADS TO THE WIRE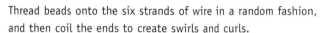

Thread beads onto the six strands of wire in a random fashion, and then coil the ends to create swirls and curls.

5 INK UP THE STAMP

Using craft glue, glue a torn piece of natural paper to the front cover of the book. Prepare the inking plate and the brayer with block-printing ink and then ink up the stamp.

6 ADD METALLIC HIGHLIGHTS

Stamp onto the papyrus paper with the stamp. Set the print aside to dry thoroughly, then glue it to the book. Add highlights to the stamped image with metallic paint to finish.

7 CREATE THE BOOKMARK

Attach the fibers to the top of the bookmark using the glue gun. Then, add a big dollop of black hot glue to the top of the fibers, ink up a portion of the stamp with ink from the metallic inkpad, and set the stamp into the hot glue. Do not press hard; just lay the stamp on the glue and wait several minutes until the glue is cool. Gently lift the stamp from the seal. Seal the ink with a clear acrylic sealer.

TEXTURE TIDBIT

JUST BE AWARE: IF YOU CHOOSE PAPERS THAT HAVE HEAVY INCLUSIONS LIKE GRASS AND TWIGS, FOR EXAMPLE, AND YOU STAMP ON THE TEXTURE, IT MAY INDENT THE SURFACE OF THE STAMP PERMANENTLY. YOU COULD STAMP ON TISSUE PAPER FIRST AND THEN LAYER THAT OVER THE HIGHLY TEXTURED SURFACE, DÉCOUPAGE-STYLE.

DRAGONFLY & ANASAZI COUGAR
JOURNALS

These artist's journals were created using small pieces of matboard with drilled holes. The inside papers are different in each journal, which I find to be a creativity-inducing element when it comes time to use them. Stamping within the books themselves lets you expand upon the cover theme or take totally new directions.

"QUICKIE"
PERSONAL JOURNAL

Instead of creating a book from scratch, you can recreate a book you already have. This is an inexpensive corrugated journal with wonderful natural pages. I added bamboo strips to the binding. Bamboo with a Mexican twist? Why not?

WHAT YOU NEED

¾" (19mm) piece of carving material

craft knife

cutting mat

pencil

fine-line permanent marker

carving tool with a small gouge blade

black archival inkpad
{ANCIENT PAGE}

archival paper or cardstock

craft glue

paper moisten-and-stick photo
corners (optional)

template for carving provided on page 122

SCRAPBOOK PHOTO CORNERS

A scrapbook has many pages of open art territory! The traditional 12" (30cm) square page offers a lot of space in which to create elements with carved stamps, from photo corners to frames, from shadow stamps to tags to decorative detail stamps that are unique and custom-designed for your own personalized artistic scrapbook presentation. You can create a photo gallery with an art gallery feel. Let's start with simple and statement-making photo corners.

STAMP CARVING

54

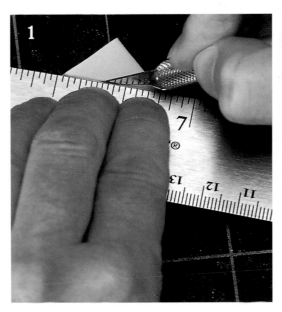

1 CREATE A TRIANGLE 👆

Cut your carving material square in half, diagonally.

2 CARVE OUT THE DESIGN 👉

Draw your design on your corner piece, or transfer it from a template. With your carving tool, cut away the design. This piece is so tiny, it works best for me to simply cut away the black lines I have drawn.

3 STAMP THE CORNERS 👉

Stamp four corners onto your paper, and allow time for them to dry. (You could also heat emboss the corners to coordinate with your page theme.)

4 ADHERE TO PAPER CORNERS ✍

Cut out the stamped corners and adhere them to the tops of ready-made corners. Alternatively, you can skip this step and glue the corners directly to your photo and scrapbook.

FRAMES AND BORDERS

Now for a confession: Where were all of my photos before I started this project? In drawers and boxes, that's where! In my mind, for months, carving a scrapbook project seemed like the easiest thing to set up. I knew I had many frames, borders, headers and other carved elements that would lend themselves to the art of scrapbooking. With just a few days left before sending all the project artwork to my editor, I found that this project was my very last.

I was having a grand old time lining up all of the stamps I had carved (photo corners, tags, borders, etc.), when all of a sudden, I hit a wall. BAM! I had all of these pieces but realized that I did not have a clue as to how to put them together! No clue and no time. To say that I was down to the wire is not extreme enough. (If only my editor knew how close it was!) Taking a hot shower to get ideas didn't help—and that always helps—so I knew I was in big trouble.

I pulled out all kinds of photos and collage materials, but every idea seemed dumb and contrived. Then, suddenly, I remembered a collaborative book exchange layout I had done, in which my theme was "Black and White." I had liked it a lot. I got out the old photos and raced to lay them out. It looked boring, and I hate boring! Dismal and not cool-looking, the black background was nothing like I had imagined. Help!

I scrambled in my studio, remembering that, on a recent visit, my Mom had bought me some art supplies and some 12" (30cm) scrapbooking pages (which I had never actually intended to use for scrapbooking). Frantically flipping through the pages, I came across two black-and-white pages that I really liked. I put them behind all the floating-in-misery photos—and presto! In that magic moment, I understood the scrapbooking craze for the first time. No wonder all of you memory artists spend a fortune on papers. I was so happy with the look! I glued things down, put waxed paper between the not-quite-dry pages, packed like a crazy person, and sent the projects on their way—to this book and to you!

This has been a glimpse into a frenzied reality that turned out just fine.

CARVING
FRAMES

In my handmade card business, I found that some designs were enhanced by carving actual frames. If you make frames in standard sizes to fit traditional photo sizes, you have an element that gives a gallery-feel to your photos—and all you have to do is ink it up and stamp. You can stamp the frames directly on the pages, or you can get an additional color by stamping on a separate piece of paper and cutting out the frame. For added dimension, float the frames on small pieces of foam tape. As for frame styles? From the most basic to the most ornate, from standard shapes and sizes to the wild and extraordinary, it's playtime in your new frame shop!

Another way to approach framing your photos is to think in terms of pieces rather than whole frames. This gives you flexibility and puts a lot of your carved images to work in ways you never imagined. Lining up individual pieces means that almost any size is easily adaptable.

CARVING
BORDERS & HEADERS

I love what is called the "shell" look, often done in wood or tin in many Mexican pieces of art. Essentially, it is a half-circle that is carved, embossed or punched to incorporate designs. They can be used at the top, bottom or side of a piece. Borders can be long carved pieces or smaller shapes that you repeat in multiples. Do the unpredictable and create interest.

CARVING
CORNERS, TAGS & SHADOWS

By carving your own photo corners you get to make them any size, color and style that you want. For an extra-large photo, try carving large corners! Carved tag and shadow stamps can be great for highlighting names or for labeling events. What if you wanted to use a shadow stamp as a corner stamp? Good thinking!

57

STAMPING ONTO FABRIC

AFTER WORKING WITH PAPER EXCLUSIVELY FOR MANY YEARS in my card business, after making thousands of cards and bookmarks, a friend of mine sensed that I was a bit "burned out," shall we say? After an art critique group meeting, she looked me straight in the eye and said: "Gloria, go home and stamp on something else, darn it!" So I did.

I took out a piece of fabric for the first time, inked up a stamp and made a banner—I loved it! I took it to her house first thing the next morning. We both smiled, and I knew that more fabric pieces were in my future. Hand-carved stamps work beautifully on fabrics. Many designers know that, too.

With the wide array of fabric inks and paints available, this frontier is wide open. Surface design on fabric can be translated into many art forms, from wearable art to wall hangings, from personal accessories to home décor items. Think big: Do your curtains or a large canvas. Think color accents: Create pillows that make a statement. Think chic: Stamp a scarf with wild, bold designs. The projects in this section will get you started.

WHAT YOU NEED

dark blue cotton fabric, about ¼ yard (23cm)

dark blue double-fold bias tape, 1 yard (91cm)

fusible webbing tape, 1½ yard (137cm)

scissors

iron

acrylic retarder (or textile medium)

foam brush

light ivory acrylic paint

white gel roller pen

templates for carvings provided on pages 122 and 123

PRAYER FLAGS

The Tibetan term for prayer flag is *Lung Ta,* which means "wind horse." The prayers printed on the flags are carried in the breeze as a blessing to all beings. The hand-carved wood blocks used to create the flags are considered very special, not simply art tools. Seeing the flags, ragged in the elements, flying from trees, temples and homes, reminds us to send wishes out to the universe. Traditional prayer flags have ragged edges for a reason. They are affected by the elements that are part of their existence, part of the release of the prayer, and also a reminder that all physical things are temporal. My Japanese version of the flags is one of many possibilities.

STAMP CARVINGS

1

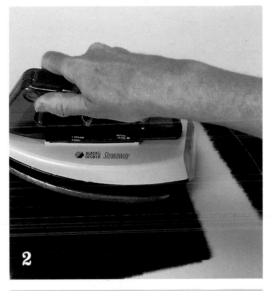

SEW EASY

FUSIBLE WEBBING WILL SHOW THROUGH
CERTAIN FABRICS, SO IF YOU'RE USING
SHEER FABRIC, BE AWARE THAT THE WEBBING
IS BEHIND THE BINDING TAPE. IF YOU DON'T
WISH TO USE THE WEBBING A SIMPLE
STRAIGHT STITCH SEWN ON TO BIND THE
FLAG PIECES AND BIAS TAPE WILL WORK
EQUALLY AS WELL.

1 IRON ON THE BIAS TAPE

Tear the fabric into three 7" x 8" (18cm x 20cm) pieces. Take
one piece of fabric and fold down 1" (3cm) from the top, making
a 7" x 7" (18cm x 18cm) square. Center the piece in the middle
of the length of bias tape. Cut two pieces of the webbing tape
to the width of the fabric. Iron down the fold, with a piece of
webbing on either side of the bias tape. This will bond the bias
tape and the fabric together.

2 CENTER THE PIECES ON THE BIAS TAPE

Iron on the remaining two pieces, one on either side of the
center piece, leaving about 1" (3cm) between the pieces.

3 STAMP THE CHARACTERS

Add the acrylic retarder to the paint, following the manufacturer's
instructions. Begin stamping with the character stamps, using
the foam brush to apply paint to the stamps. Stamp one character
in the center of each fabric square.

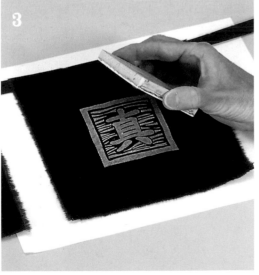

2

3

STAMPING ON FABRIC REQUIRES PUTTING SOMETHING
UNDER THE FABRIC TO PROTECT TABLE OR FLOOR
SURFACES. I USE PAPER AT TIMES, BUT USUALLY I USE
PLASTIC SHEETS THAT I MAKE OUT OF CUT PLASTIC
TRASH BAGS OR CHEAP PLASTIC TABLECLOTHS FROM
DOLLAR STORES.

4 STAMP THE OTHER IMAGES 👆

Stamp one shell image onto the binding tape between each square of fabric, and stamp three shells on both ends. Stamp the flower image on either side of the characters.

5 WRITE THE TRANSLATIONS 👉

If you like, write the translations of the characters in white gel pen below each character on each flag. When using a gel pen on fabric, it helps to write very slowly. The translations for my characters are *beauty, gratitude* and *simplicity*.

THE COLOR OF A PRAYER

FIVE COLORS ARE COMMON TO THE PRAYER FLAGS OF TIBETAN BUDDHISM BECAUSE THE NUMBER FIVE ITSELF REPRESENTS NOT ONLY THE FIVE MEDITATION BUDDHAS BUT ALSO THE FIVE WISDOMS, THE FIVE MENTAL ATTRIBUTES AND THE FIVE PHYSICAL ELEMENTS. INDIVIDUALLY, WHITE REPRESENTS CLOUD; YELLOW, EARTH; RED, FIRE; BLUE, SKY; AND GREEN, WATER.

TIBETAN SYMBOLS
PRAYER FLAG

It was a special experience for me to try to capture the feeling of a Tibetan prayer flag with my own carvings. (Special thanks to Kel Toomb for allowing me to carve my images based on his carved renditions.) I explored different color tones of the traditional style, and I felt a spiritual satisfaction in trying to honor this sacred means of communication.

AFRICAN ADINKRA SYMBOLS
PRAYER FLAG

So many wonderful commercially printed fabrics are available. Some artists dye and print everything they work with; I enjoy playing with all kinds of fabrics and have collected many pieces over the years. This flag features three African Adinkra symbols, which are translated as "good living," "strength" and "enjoy yourself." I used small commercial stamps (Chronicle) and larger blocks of the same designs that I carved.

HAPPY HOLIDAYS
FLAGS

Just as there are fabric prayer flags, so can there be paper versions. I made this holiday variation with small papers, and I envision this as a type of garland in a tree. You could create prayer flags for many different occasions. Celebrate a birthday and stamp the birthday person's name. Create a memorial prayer flag for someone who has passed away. Commemorate a personally declared accomplishment or milestone.

WHAT YOU NEED

lightweight fabric cut to:

  36" × 10" (91cm × 25cm)

  36" × 4" (91cm × 10cm), two pieces

sewing thread to match fabric

black sewing thread

needle

scissors

black inkpad {VERSACRAFT}

scrap paper

reinker for black inkpad

iron (to heat set)

red inkpad {VERSACRAFT}

black grosgrain ribbon,
⅜" (10mm) wide, 2 yards (183cm)

silver leaf beads, eight

piece of bamboo, 1½" (4cm)
diameter × 22" (56cm)

black silk cording

wire, 6" (15cm)

large square silver button

sewing machine (optional)

templates for carvings provided on page 123

BAMBOO BANNER

In creating this banner, I wanted a design that was very simple and fluid in a breezy kind of way. Hang this piece where it can flutter. By nature, bamboo is strong yet flexible—not to mention, it brings good luck! When creating your own bamboo banner, let the bamboo "design" the dimensions because no two poles will ever be exactly the same. Divide your pieces of fabric accordingly.

STAMP CARVINGS

64

1 STAMP ON THE NARROW PANELS ☞

Sew a 3" (8cm) channel on each of the fabric pieces for the bamboo, leaving a total length of 30" (76cm) for each piece. Trim off any excess fabric. Lay out the three pieces to make the composition easier to see. On the left piece, stamp two leaves near the bottom. Stamp a series of leaves on the right piece, using a scrap-paper mask if desired.

2 STAMP THE CENTER PIECE ☞

Ink up the large stamp with the inkpad, tapping in multiple directions to avoid getting any lines. You may need to add ink from the reinker bottle because this stamp will take a large amount of ink. Stamp onto the center panel three times in three different directions with the same large stamp. Overlapping the image is fine. After all the panels are dry, heat-set them with an iron.

3 SEW THE RIBBON PIECES ☞

Stamp your personal signature stamp in red in the bottom-right corner of the center piece. Cut the length of ribbon into two lengths of 1 yard (91cm) each. Sew three leaf beads onto one end of one piece. Wrap the piece around the bamboo and pin it together. Sew the ribbon together to create a loop, and sew on a bead where the ribbon is sewn together. Repeat for the other ribbon.

WHAT IS "MASKING?"

WHEN YOU WANT TO GET A LAYERED LOOK THAT "HIDES" PART OF THE IMAGE, YOU CAN CREATE A PAPER MASK SIMPLY BY STAMPING YOUR IMAGE ON A PIECE OF SCRAP PAPER AND CUTTING IT OUT PRECISELY ALONG THE PERIMETER LINE. PLACE THE CUTOUT OVER YOUR PREVIOUSLY STAMPED IMAGE, INK UP WHATEVER STAMP YOU WANT TO USE AND STAMP PARTLY ON THE PAPER AND PARTLY ON THE FABRIC. WHEN YOU LIFT OFF THE PAPER MASK, YOU CAN SEE THE INTERESTING RESULT!

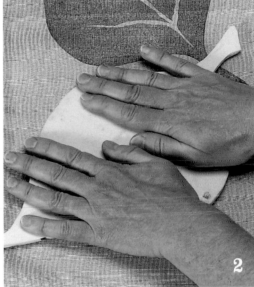

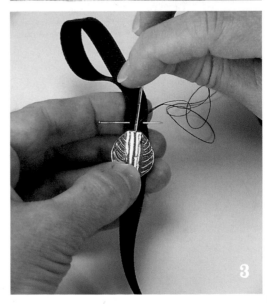

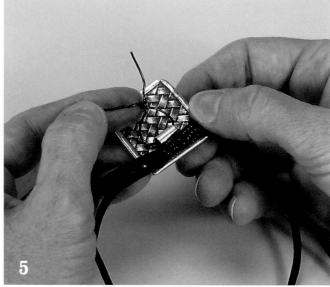

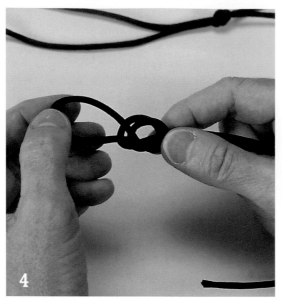

4 TIE THE SILK CORD

Cut two lengths of silk cord, 24" (61cm) each. Double up each piece and tie a knot at the loop end. The loop that is created must fit around the bamboo.

5 CREATE A HANGER

Using the piece of wire, wire the two cord ends (four strands) together, thread each end of the wire through the large silver bead, and then twist the ends of wire together to create a hanger.

6 LAY OUT ALL OF THE PIECES

Trim the ends of the wire, if necessary. Lay out all of your pieces in the order that they will be going on the bamboo.

7 SLIDE THE PIECES ONTO THE BAMBOO

Thread the pieces onto the bamboo in the order in which you have them laid out. Once you have all the pieces in place, your banner is ready to hang, either on a wall or suspended in an open space.

TOUCH UP

YOU CAN TOUCH UP SPOTS THAT WERE MADE BY SHIFTING OR THAT WERE MISSED, USING A DETAIL BRUSH AND THE REINKER INKS, ACTING AS PAINT.

IMAGINE
BANNER

From bamboo to copper pipes, from vertical to horizontal, from images to words—imagine the possibilities! Inspirational words are good to have in our lives, and when you make words into works of art, you get to see them as well as reflect upon them. Here, the copper pipes were cut at the hardware store, and the letters came from an alphabet set designed and carved by yours truly.

HAND-CARVED

DO YOU WANT A CARVED HAND STAMP LIKE THE ONE I USED AS MY SIGNATURE ON THE BAMBOO BANNER? OR, A MORE TRUE-TO-LIFE ONE LIKE THE ONE USED HERE? GREAT! PUT ONE OF YOUR HANDS DOWN ON A PIECE OF COPY PAPER AND TRACE IT WITH A REGULAR PENCIL. GO OVER THE OUTLINE TO SMOOTH THE LINES AND DARKEN THE PENCIL. DRAW YOUR OWN SYMBOL IN THE CENTER. TRANSFER THIS IMAGE TO A CARVING BLOCK, THEN CARVE AND STAMP. TO MAKE A SMALLER VERSION, REDUCE THE TRACING OF YOUR HAND ON A COPIER AND CREATE A CARVING FROM THE REDUCTION. THIS CAN THEN SERVE AS YOUR SIGNATURE. NO ONE ELSE HAS A HAND JUST LIKE YOURS.

67

WHAT YOU NEED

muslin, two pieces torn to
7" × 12" (18cm × 30cm)

needle and thread
(or sewing machine)

scrap paper

black inkpad for fabric {VERSACRAFT}

iron (to heat set)

foam brushes

acrylic paints: red, magenta,
pink, yellow and orange

small alphabet rubber stamp set

black inkpad for tags {STAZON}

copper or glass tags

bulbs and seeds

colored netting, ½ yard (46cm)

ivory grosgrain ribbon, 24" (61cm)

copper wire, two 10" (25cm) lengths

round-nosed pliers

templates for carvings provided on page 123

BOTANICAL BAG

This folk-art-style bag, with its old coarse gunnysack material, looks like the type of thing that would have carried potatoes, coffee beans or any number of items in an old-fashioned Western general store. The labels on the bags are decorative as well as utilitarian. Botanical cloth bags can be made in any size to hold all kinds of wonderful, fragrant and organic things! Try burlap and other textured fabrics for a "genuine article" look. From bulbs and seeds to soaps, herbs, teas, potpourri, incense, spices, candles, aromatherapy oils, perfumes and more, this project creates a heavenly presentation for an earthy, natural gift.

68

STAMP CARVINGS

BULBS & SEEDS

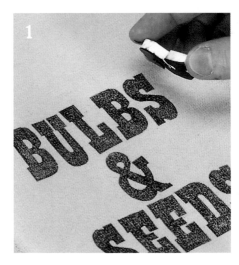

1 STAMP LETTERS AT THE BOTTOM

Sew together three sides of the muslin either by hand or with a sewing machine. Keep the frayed edges as the outside edges of the bag to enhance the look. Place scrap paper inside the bag to prepare for stamping. Stamp the row of letters at the bottom of the bag first, to make positioning easier. Then follow with the remainging letters above. Heat set the bag with an iron when the ink is dry.

2 STAMP THE PETALED FLOWER

For the flower's center, use a foam brush to apply yellow and orange paint to the round stamp. Stamp the flower center about 2" (5cm) above the word BULBS. Place a piece of scrap paper over the letters to act as a mask when stamping the petals. Use the foam brush to apply pink and magenta paint to the petal stamp and stamp the petals individually around the flower center, adding more paint as needed.

3 STAMP THE TULIPS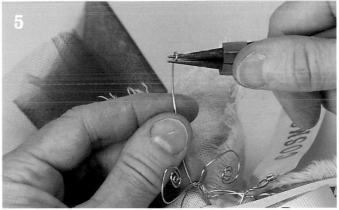

Finish with two stamped tulips on either side of the ampersand in red acrylic paint.

4 ADD THE BULB VARIETIES

Stamp the names of the bulbs or seeds onto the copper (or glass) tags with the small alphabet set and the StazOn black inkpad.

5 TIE-OFF WITH WIRE

Gather the bulbs and seeds inside the piece of netting, then stuff it into the bag, letting the netting stick out of the top. Tie the bag shut with the length of ribbon, and then twist on the copper or glass tags with a length of copper wire. Use the round-nosed pliers to create spirals for the wire ends.

STAMPING ONTO TEXTURE

WHEN USING A MATERIAL LIKE BURLAP, WHICH HAS A LOOSE, OPEN-WEAVE, YOU WILL HAVE BETTER LUCK USING SOLID, CHUNKY-TYPE STAMPS RATHER THAN STAMPS WITH A LOT OF FINE DETAIL. IF NECESSARY, PAINT OVER DESIGNS TO GET MORE COLOR SATURATION.

WHAT YOU NEED

black silk blouse

any dye inkpad
(to make a mask)

fabric acrylics: Super Copper,
Metallic Bronze (LUMIERE)

removable tape

foam brushes, two

scissors

scrap paper

iron (to heat set)

templates for carvings provided
on page 123

SECOND LIFE SILK BLOUSE

Bargain shopping at thrift stores and yard sales and receiving hand-me-downs from classy people is just plain fun! I also like giving a second life to my own clothes that have become either "tired" or slightly damaged in some way: a splash of bleach perhaps or fading that would love some new color. Whether hats, shoes, blouses, jackets, skirts or vests, when you pay just a couple of dollars—like I did for this black silk blouse—you can play with it, then wear it and look and feel like a million bucks.

STAMP CARVINGS

70

1 APPLY PAINT TO THE STAMP

Wash and iron your garment before beginning to eliminate all wrinkles. Set a piece of scrap paper under the layer of fabric that you are going to stamp. Using the foam brushes, dab paint on the stamp with areas of both colors of paint. This placement of color is completely random.

2 STAMP ALONG THE BLOUSE BOTTOM

Stamp with the same stamp along the bottom of the shirt. Leave one space blank. We will be stamping the other leaf image in the open space.

3 STAMP OVER A MASK

Cut two pieces of paper to mask the last two stamped images on either side of the open space. Secure the paper with removable tape. Brush paint on the other stamp in the same way as the first and stamp the image in the open space.

4 TOUCH UP MISSED SPOTS

If some areas are missing fabric paint or you want to highlight some areas with contrasting colors, you can go back and touch them up with a brush. I like the look of Lumieres when they are not too fussed over.

5 HEAT SET THE STAMPED IMAGES

Stamp the last image onto a piece of scrap paper with black ink and then cut a portion of it out to act as a mask. Stamp the image on the top right portion of the shirt. Then set the mask on top of the image and stamp it again. Heat set the dried images with an iron, following the manufacturer's directions.

WHAT YOU NEED

fabric strips, torn to 8" × 2" (20cm × 5cm),
three hardware cloth, 11½" × 5" (29cm × 13cm)

wood dowels (square):

⅜" × 12" (10mm × 30cm), three

⅛" × 6" (3mm × 15cm), three

wood cube, 1½" (4cm)

glass tealight holders, two

black inkpad {VERSACRAFT}

black inkpad {STAZON}

black wood stain

cloth rag

protective gloves

black glass paint
{AIR-DRY PERMENAMEL BY DELTA}

permanent marker

pencil

beads

bronze-colored wire

five-minute epoxy

detail brush

foam brush

wire cutters

round-nosed pliers

tealight candles

iron (to heat set)

template for carving provided on page 123

CANDLE TOWER

Candlelight . . . peaceful and warm, romantic and meditative—I love to have candles in my home and in my life. This project is meant to be playful. I played with fabric, glass, metal and wood in this Candle Towers project. For anyone who loves creating with candles, this is a wonderful chance to explore design. Start with shapes, sizes and colors that you like working with. I started with green glass cubes and built my concept from there. You might start with blue glass globes, floating candles or ethnic stoneware, and take this idea in a new direction. Make large groupings and alter the sizes for impact. Take my ideas, add your own, loosen up, be creative and bask in the glow!

STAMP CARVING

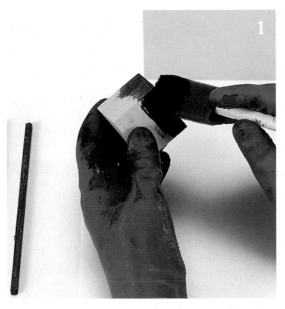

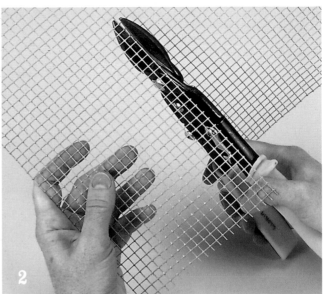

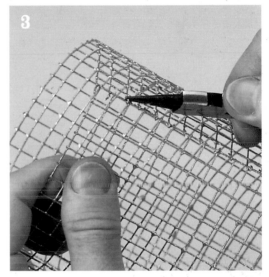

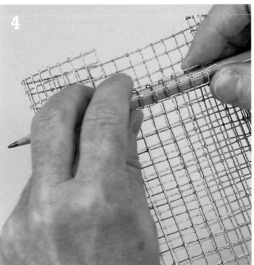

1   STAIN THE WOOD

Stain all of the wood pieces with the black stain. Brush on with a foam brush and then rub off with a rag.

2   PREPARE HARDWARE CLOTH

Cut one short end of the hardware cloth so that the wire ends are loose (like fringe), and cut the long ends so that the edges are clean.

3   CREATE A CYLINDER

Roll the hardware cloth into a cylinder shape and bend the "fringe-end" wires around the opposite short side to connect the two ends.

4   ROLL DOWN FRONT SECTION

Stand the cylinder up and, with the connected seam at the back, visually find the front, center opposite it. Mark the center with a marker. Count out three squares from either side of the center, mark those spots and then cut down eight squares from each mark. Roll down this tab over a pencil.

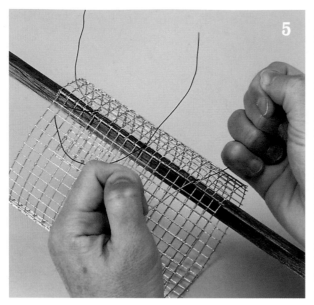

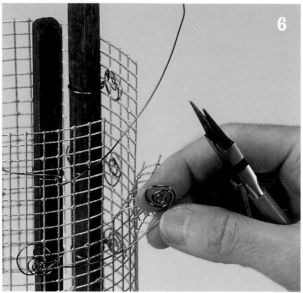

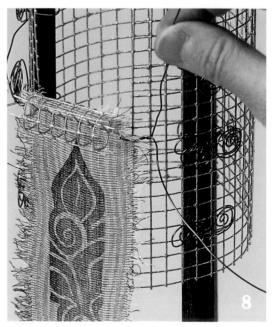

5 ATTACH THE FIRST DOWEL

Cut nine pieces of wire to about 10" (25cm) each. Position one of the larger dowels 1¾" (4cm) above the top of the cylinder, at the seam in the back. Count down five squares from the top, thread a piece of wire into the cylinder, around the dowel and back out again, and then twist it tightly. Repeat with another piece of wire, five squares up from the bottom, and a third piece centered between the first two.

6 ATTACH THE OTHER DOWELS

Coil all the ends of the wire with the round-nosed pliers to create random swirls. Repeat with the other two dowels, creating a tripod. Position the other two dowels about five squares in from the rolled-down opening, or wherever the balance seems best.

7 STAMP THE FABRIC

Stamp the three torn pieces of fabric with the stamp and the black VersaCraft inkpad. Heat set the image with an iron when dry.

8 THREAD FABRIC WITH WIRE

Cut six lengths of wire, about 10" (25cm) each. Fold the top of one piece of fabric back about ¼" (6mm). Poke the wire through at each corner, and twist the wire once or twice at the top. Thread the wire through the cylinder to attach and hang the fabric piece under the rolled-down portion.

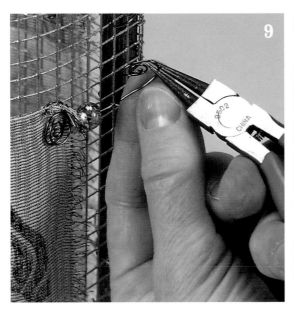

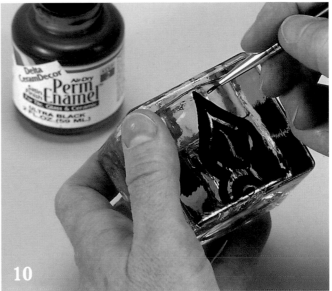

9 ADD BEADS TO THE WIRE

Add the remaining fabric in the same fashion, centering the other two pieces between the dowels. Thread beads onto the strands of wire and coil the ends.

10 STAMP ONTO THE GLASS

Insert the short dowel pieces horizontally through the cylinder to create a shelf. Stamp onto the glass tealight holder with black StazOn ink. When dry, go over the design with a detail brush and the black glass paint.

11 STAMP ONTO THE WOOD CUBE

Stamp the stained wood cube using black VersaCraft ink. Use just the top portion of the stamp for the design element.

12 ADD A WIRE EMBELLISHMENT

Cut one last piece of wire to about 8" (20cm) and thread one bead onto it. With the bead in the center, coil the wire on either side to create an S-shape. Adhere this piece to the stamped side of the cube with epoxy. Go over the entire tall tower and epoxy each place where the bronze wire is wrapped around wood to make sure the entire piece is stable. Add tealight candles after the epoxy is dry. There is a flame involved, so please display the tower carefully.

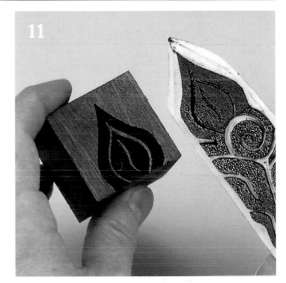

WHAT YOU NEED

light-weight fabric,
two pieces 12" × 12" (30cm × 30cm)

black inkpad {VERSACRAFT}

red inkpad {VERSACRAFT}

fabric acrylics: Super Copper
and Metallic Bronze {LUMIERE}

iron (to heat set)

fusible webbing, 12" × 12" (30cm x 30cm),
two pieces

plain paper, 11" × 11" (28cm × 28cm)
and 10" × 10" (25cm × 25cm)

scissors

craft glue

heavy-weight decorative paper,
4" (10cm) square and
3½" (9cm) square

round-nosed pliers

black wire, two 10" (25cm) lengths

hot glue gun

hot glue stick, red

metallic pigment ink
{COLORBOX PAINTBOX 2}

assorted beads

templates for carvings provided
on page 123

MASU BOX

In Japan, the art of packaging and presentation is just
that—an art. This Masu (meaning "measure") box is a
simple form of paper folding. I have added the element
of fabric to what is traditionally a paper project, but if
you prefer using paper, your hand-carved stamps will look just as spectacular on the
paper of your choice. You start with two squares. There are folds, but no cuts. When you
have completed your Masu box as a work of art in itself, you can add to the experience
by placing something special inside: the complete gift to a friend—or to yourself!

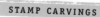
STAMP CARVINGS

1 STAMP A PATTERN 👉

Stamp the two 12" (30cm) square fabrics with your carved stamps, using the red and black inkpads. If you want the pattern on your box to end up diagonally, stamp the pattern parallel to the fabric sides; if you want the pattern on the box to be straight, stamp diagonally. The way I have stamped this piece, the design will appear diagonal after being folded. This is the top part of the box, so it will be 11" (28cm) square after being trimmed. I stamped a black piece of fabric with Lumiere paints for the base and will trim it to 10" (25cm) square.

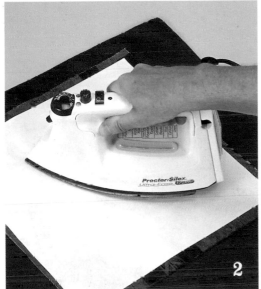

2 BOND THE FABRIC TO PAPER 👉

Heat set the stamped pieces of fabric with an iron after the paints have dried. Bond a piece of fusible webbing to the two pieces of paper, trim off any excess webbing, and then bond the paper to the pieces of fabric. Be careful not to burn the paper. Iron on both sides.

3 BEGIN FOLDING THE BOX TOP 👉

Trim off the excess fabric from the paper. Beginning with the larger piece (the box top), create folds according to the first ten steps in the diagrams here.

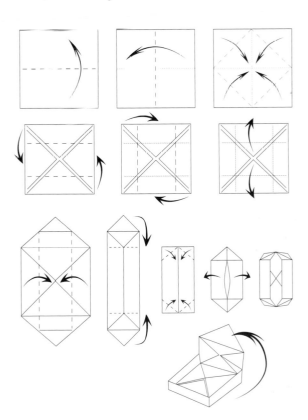

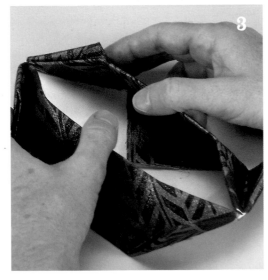

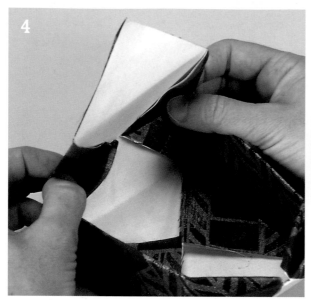

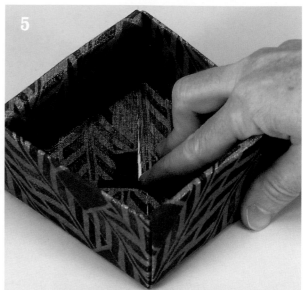

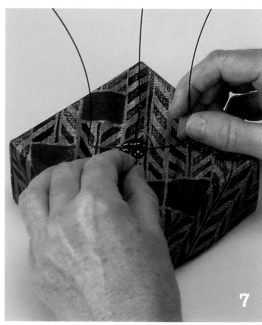

4 PULL OUT THE FLAPS

Pull the flaps out from under the box (See diagram step 11.)

5 FOLD THE FLAPS TO THE INSIDE

Fold the flaps inside the box, and crease with your fingers all the way around the edge to form a nice crisp shape.

6 CREATE THE BOX AND LID LINERS

Repeat steps 3–5 for the smaller piece (the box bottom). I like to glue the flaps down inside the box pieces at this point. Take the two trimmed pieces of decorative paper (or matboard) and glue theses pieces into the inside top and bottom of the box with generous amounts of craft glue. These pieces give the interior of the box a beautiful look and add to its stability.

7 ATTACH WIRE TO THE TOP

Use the round-nosed pliers to bend each wire piece in two places, about 2" (5cm) apart, creating a U-shape with corners. Place a small dollop of red hot glue on top of the box. While the glue is hot, set up the two pieces of wire in the glue so that they form an X-shape. Hold in place until the glue cools.

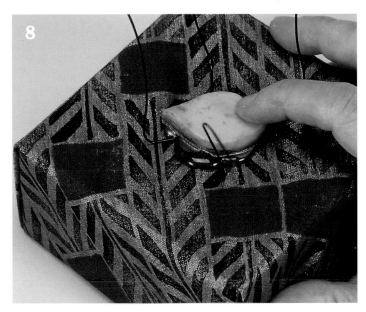

8 ADD A HOT GLUE SEAL

Secure the pieces with another large dollop of red hot glue from the glue gun, and then set a stamp that has metallic pigment ink on it into the hot glue. Let the stamp set until the glue cools, then remove the stamp.

9 ADD BEADS TO FINISH

Thread beads onto the four strands of wire, about halfway up each strand. Use the round-nosed pliers to coil the ends into spirals and make various bends and curves in the beaded portions to finish.

BIGGER IS BETTER

THE REASON I START OUT WITH FABRIC PIECES A LITTLE LARGER THAN NEEDED IS TO ACCOUNT FOR THE MATERIAL SHIFTING AS YOU IRON OR GLUE IT DOWN. IT'S MUCH EASIER TO TRIM OFF A LITTLE EXCESS, THAN TO TRY AND KEEP EVERYTHING ALIGNED PERFECTLY.

MASU BOX
VARIATIONS

Traditionally, these boxes are made with paper, so I wanted to share some paper versions with you. Using beautiful Japanese papers or grasscloth connects you to the box's origin, and creating with recycled or edgy art papers takes you to new places. Think of the whole box as a canvas. Give surprises inside and out. Make several sizes and nest them together.

79

WHAT YOU NEED

base print fabric, 9½" x 13" (24cm × 33cm), two pieces

interfacing, two pieces, 9" × 12½" (23cm × 32cm)

thick felt, 9" × 12½" (23cm × 32cm) (optional)

sewing machine

various pieces torn fabric in coordinating prints

iron

black inkpad {VERSACRAFT}

red inkpad {VERSACRAFT}

fabric paints: red, silver and pewter {LUMIERE}

foam brushes

tote bag

jumbo snaps, six

needle and thread for sewing snaps

metallic decorative fibers

assorted charms or other embellishments

templates for carvings provided on pages 123 and 124

QUICK-CHANGE ART QUILT TOTE

I am a one-purse woman, mostly because I can't be bothered to switch out the contents. But sometimes it is just plain boring picking up the same-old-same-old bag. So, how about a tote that lets you keep things inside and, with a few big snaps, change the whole look on the outside? Hook-and-loop closures could work, too, but there is just something irresistible about big snaps. Keep a few panels handy and make a quick change when the mood or occasion calls for a statement other than "useful."

STAMP CARVINGS

80

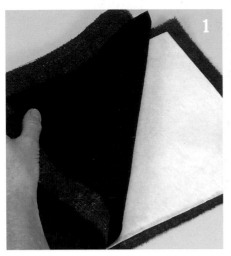

IT'S A SNAP!

COLOR THE POINTS IN THE SNAPS
(ALREADY SEWN ON THE PANEL) WITH
A BLACK MARKER AND THEN PRESS
THE PANEL PIECE ONTO THE TOTE
TO MARK WHERE THE BASES OF THE
SNAPS SHOULD GO.

1 CREATE A FABRIC BASE

Decide on a theme, and then pick fabric and stamps accordingly.
Layer interfacing and felt between two pieces of base print fabric,
to make a nice, stiff panel. Sew all the pieces together around
the perimeter and set this panel aside.

2 STAMP ONTO FABRIC STRIPS

Tear your assorted prints of fabric into strips of various lengths.
Here, the width of my strips is about 2" (5cm). Stamp with
an assortment of stamps onto the strips. Use both the inkpads
and fabric paints, which you can apply with a foam brush to
your stamps. Be spontaneous and not overly planned with
this stamping.

3 CREATE THE PANEL

Lay out your stamped fabric strips on top of the red base fabric
in a composition that you find pleasing, and pin down the
pieces for sewing. Sew the strips to the panel and embellish
the front with wire, beads and decorative fibers.

4 SEW ON THE SNAPS

Sew snaps on the back of the panel, three on top and three on
the bottom. Position the panel on the tote to see where the
snap bases should be sewn. (See *It's a Snap*, above.) Sew them
on the bag, three on top and three on the bottom. Snap the
panel in place to complete.

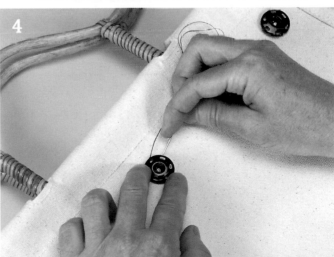

MORE IS MORE

GO AHEAD AND STAMP MORE STRIPS THAN YOU NEED
BECAUSE YOU HAVE ALL THE MATERIALS OUT AND
HANDY. EVERYTHING THAT IS LEFT OVER IS GREAT
TO HAVE FOR OTHER ART PROJECTS.

AFRICAN
BAG

African textiles are so rich in history and cultural stories. From mudcloth with very literal earth tones to highly colored woven pieces, the range is vast. I have a fabulous mudcloth vest that is long and elegant—a gift from my Mom. I love wearing it with turquoise jewelry, and now I have a bag that goes with it!

NAVAJO
BAG

If a room has an old Navajo blanket in it, I feel at home. Books on Navajo weaving are great to inspire designs. These stamps are variations of elements found in different vintage rugs. The red linen comes from a good shopping day in Santa Fe, the Mexican button is the real thing, and the conchos are cheap replicas from a craft store in Missouri. Hey, you do the best you can!

FISH & WAVES
BAG

You would think a color palette for
fish and waves might consist of blues
and greens, but not this time! It is
good to challenge the predictable
and make your own statement. Yes,
a spiral can become a wave!

NAVAJO
JACKET

The quick-change concept does not
need to be limited to tote bags. I dyed
this thrift-store denim jacket teal
to acquire a new "canvas" and,
using the same big snaps that
were used on the bags, made
it possible to change the
artistic panel to suit my
mood. This jacket makes
a great companion to the
Navajo bag.

83

ALTERNATIVE SURFACES

ONCE I WENT FROM STAMPING ON PAPER TO FABRIC, I knew a "next step" was inevitable. My art-group friends got an idea to sign up for a class at the university craft studio in a medium totally foreign to all of us. When we saw a brochure advertising a class in handmade tiles, we knew that we had found what we were looking for!

For the first class I decided to take along some of my hand carved stamps to see if I could push them into the clay and make tiles with them. My prediction was that they would make the biggest mess. I thought they would get shmooshed into the clay, bits and pieces would get stuck in them like shoes in mud, and cleaning them out would probably take the whole night. Guess what? No mess, just magic! My teacher looked over my shoulder as the stamp released easily and said, "Very cool. We are breaking new ground here."

This experience changed the way I thought about carving. I saw real potential for texture. When you carve into the block deeply, you get a notably raised effect in clay.

Experimenting with polymer clay is a great way to get this experience at home without the need for a major kiln setup. In addition to dabbling with clay, we will explore alternative surfaces for stamping in this chapter. Gourds sound wonderful—how about leather? Wood, river rocks, glass—you name it because you love it. In this section, let's open up the possibilities.

LEATHER BRACELET

Wearing leather accessories is fun! Leather comes in so many different colors and varieties, from tan to red to black; from thin to thick; and rough, brushed and smooth. Polymer clay buttons are easy to make and have so many applications. Here we use one as a bracelet fastener. The leather bracelet in this project is comfortable to wear, and once you create one, you probably will want more—so will your friends!

STAMP CARVINGS

86

1 STAMP ONTO THE LEATHER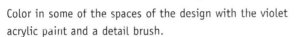

Using scissors, round the corners of the strip of leather. Then, using the black inkpad, stamp onto the strip with the large stamp. Don't stamp the design all the way to the end; leave some space to stamp again with just a bit of the image.

2 COLOR IN DETAILS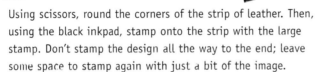

Color in some of the spaces of the design with the violet acrylic paint and a detail brush.

3 STAMP A CLAY BUTTON

Roll out a small bit of conditioned polymer clay, and cut out a square button shape. Stamp into the clay button with a small stamp of your choice, using the purple mica inkpad.

PROPER CONDITIONING

BEFORE WORKING WITH POLYMER CLAY AND STAMPING INTO IT, IT IS IMPORTANT TO CONDITION THE CLAY BY WORKING IT OVER AND OVER IN YOUR HANDS OR BY RUNNING IT THROUGH A CLAY-DEDICATED PASTA MACHINE MULTIPLE TIMES. THIS MAKES THE CLAY SOFT AND PLIABLE.

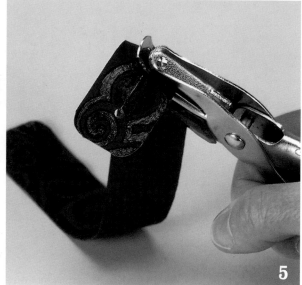

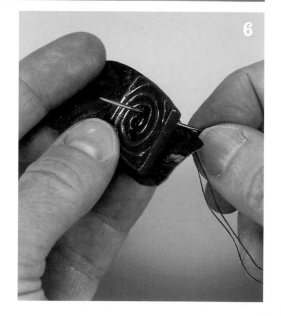

4 ADD MICA TO THE BUTTON

Rub a bit of mica powder onto the button, if you like, to add interest. Then using a stylus, make two holes in the button. Turn over the button and do the same on the back, making the openings smooth and flat.

5 CUT A BUTTON HOLE

Bake the button according to the manufacturer's instructions, then let it cool. On the end of the bracelet that will have the opening for the button, punch a hole with the ⅛" (3mm) hole punch, about ½" (13mm) from the end. Then, use the craft knife to make a small slit, parallel to the length of the strip, that is just slightly larger than the width of the button. At the other end of the cut, make one more ⅛" (3mm) hole.

6 SEW ON THE BUTTON

On the end of the bracelet opposite the slit, position the button so that it is almost at the end of the leather strip. Sew it on with black thread. Tie it off under the button to avoid having a knot on the inside of the bracelet, which can make wearing the bracelet uncomfortable.

THESE BRACELETS WOULD BE FUN WITH OTHER EMBELLISHMENTS SUCH AS BEADS AND MORE BUTTONS, AS DECORATIVE ADDITIONS. I WOULD LINE THE BRACELETS EITHER WITH ANOTHER PIECE OF LEATHER GLUED ON, OR FABRIC TO KEEP THE BEAD AND EMBELLISHMENT THREADS FROM BEING A BOTHER ON YOUR WRIST.

OTHER BRACELETS

Have fun with different colors and stamp combinations! The possibilities are wide open. How about wearing several leather bracelets at the same time? Or cut a longer piece of leather and make a choker.

ART BUTTONS

Make polymer clay buttons galore! The more polymer techniques you know, the more fun you will have. Buttons are for wearable art, art quilts, altered books, art books and closures of all kinds. Buttons can have the traditional two or four holes, but what about three—or none at all? I stamped the faces of some buttons and, after baking them, used five-minute epoxy to adhere coiled wire loops to the backs for easy sewing.

89

WHAT YOU NEED

black inkpad {STAZON}

river rock, medium size

fine-point black
permanent marker

assorted yarns

hot glue stick, red

hot glue gun

craft glue

copper wire, 12" (30cm), two lengths

Mexican Sun stamp
{CHRONICLE}

metallic pigment inkpad
{PAINTBOX}

sealer of your choice

beads and sequins

round-nosed pliers

metallic paints {LUMIERE}

template for carving provided
on page 124

RIVER ROCK

The smoothness of river rocks gives us a stamping
canvas a bit out of the ordinary. Go to a local garden
center or better yet, trek the river's edge along the Rio Grande (or any nearby river or
stream) to collect river rocks, large and small. You will discover a spectrum of natural
shades from grays and tans to rose tones, that have their own stories after countless
years of tumbling to become the smooth stone in your hand. Whether you simply stamp
an Asian image on the stone to add to your meditation fountain or jazz up a Mexican-
themed rock with yarns and beads to create a little sculptural piece, river rocks rock!

STAMP CARVING

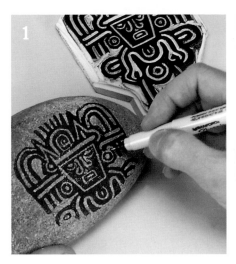

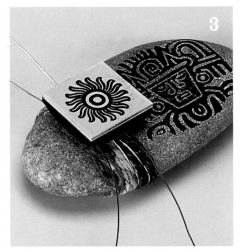

1 STAMP ONTO THE ROCK

Ink up the stamp with the black inkpad. Stamp onto the rock, gently "wrapping" the stamp over the edges to conform to the rock's shape. Touch up any missed spots with a permanent marker, if you wish.

2 WRAP WITH YARN

Secure the first length of yarn to the back of the rock with the glue gun. Lightly apply craft glue around the rock where the yarn will be. Tightly wrap the yarn around the rock several times, lining it up neatly as you wrap. Secure the end and the next color with the glue gun, then repeat until you have all of the colors you want.

3 ADD A HOT GLUE SEAL

Wrap the two lengths of copper wire around the yarn portion and twist twice. Add a hot glue seal over the twisted wire and yarn with the red glue stick and the glue gun. Ink up a Mexican design art stamp with metallic ink and set the stamp in the hot glue. Let it stand for several minutes, until cool. Seal with acrylic sealer, if desired.

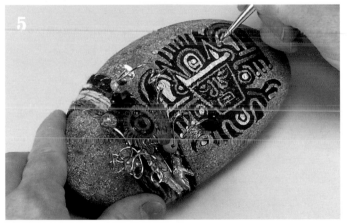

4 CREATE BEADED COILS

Add beads to the loose strands of wire and create coils on the ends using the pliers.

5 FINISH WITH HIGHLIGHTS

Add highlights to the stamped image with copper, silver and gold metallic paints.

OTHER IDEAS

A GREAT LOOK FOR A RIVER ROCK IS THE SIMPLICITY OF AN ORIENTAL ZEN GARDEN. FIND A VERY FLAT RIVER ROCK, AND STAMP A MEANINGFUL SYMBOL ON IT. USE PERMANENT INK, WHICH WILL GIVE YOUR RIVER ROCK THE VERSATILITY TO BE INDOORS OR OUTDOORS IN A FOUNTAIN OR GARDEN. I BUY LOVELY PALE GREEN ROCKS FROM A LOCAL GARDEN SHOP, STAMP DIFFERENT SYMBOLS ON THEM, AND GIVE THEM AS GIFTS INSIDE SMALL HANDMADE MASU BOXES (SEE PROJECT ON PAGE 76).

CERAMIC TILE

Using two commercial ceramic tiles—one for the artwork and the other as a mount for the piece—we have artwork that can be displayed either on a stand or on the wall. This project is presented as a single piece, but imagine the impact of a grouping. Be creative with your choices of tissue papers and explore the possibilities that present themselves with the transparent nature of the paper. The contrast between the texture of the tumbled piece and the gloss of the black tile enhances the impact. Natural slate also makes a great-looking tile piece, especially suited for Southwest designs. Or, if you're having dreams of France, how about a Lascaux Cave piece with carved horses?

STAMP CARVING

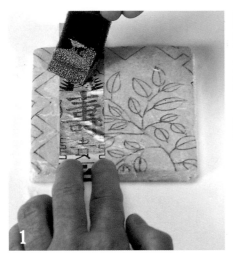

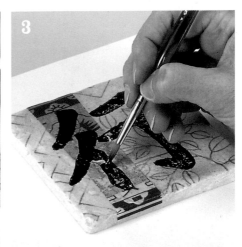

1 APPLY PAPER TO TILE

Trim one piece of paper to the size of your white tile. Adhere it to the front of the tile using a foam brush and découpage medium. Brush the medium directly on the tile, add the paper, smooth it down and allow to dry. Next, layer a strip to go along the left side, on top of that. Set aside to dry.

2 STAMP ONTO THE TILE

Stamp onto the dried, découpaged tile with the carved stamp, using the black inkpad. The image may be "sketchy" because of the texture of the découpage layers. If you like the way it looks, leave it alone!

3 PAINT OVER THE IMAGE

If you feel the image needs to be enhanced, darken it further with the black enamel paint, using the detail brush.

4 ADD THE TRANSLATION

Write the translation of the character on the side of the tile, using a permanent marker or a pen made especially for writing on glass or ceramic. The character I've used here translates to *journey*.

5 GLUE TILES TOGETHER

Using five-minute epoxy, adhere the stamped tile to the center of the larger, black tile. Place the dots or lines of epoxy glue at least 1" (3cm) in on the tile, so that it doesn't ooze out when you press down. Set it aside to cure.

6 ADHERE A WIRE HANGER

Create a hanger for the back by cutting a piece of picture-hanging wire, coiling the ends with pliers and then gluing them to the tile back with small puddles of epoxy.

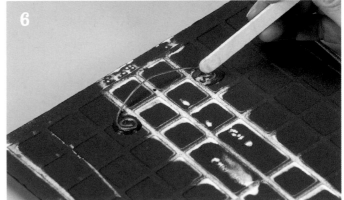

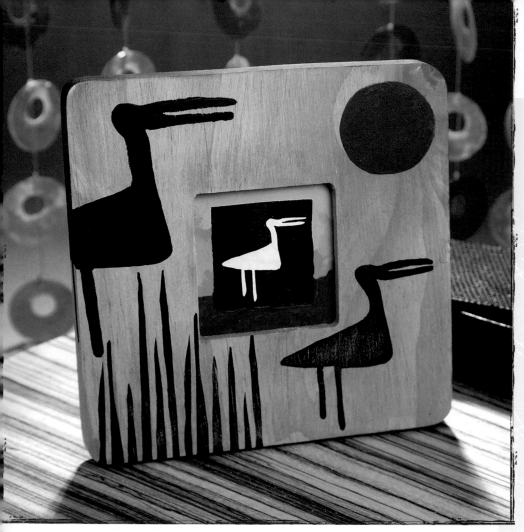

WHAT YOU NEED

protective gloves

mustard-toned wood stain

unfinished wooden frame, 8" × 8" (20cm × 20cm)

foam brush

rag

black inkpad {VERSACRAFT}

red inkpad {VERSACRAFT}

acrylic paint: turquoise, rust and black

detail paint brush

cream-colored cardstock

black inkpad {COLORBOX}

clear embossing powder

heat gun

templates for carvings provided on page 124

SOUTHWEST BY FAR EAST FRAME

Unfinished wood presents a great stamping opportunity. I designed this project around a simple square wooden frame and a square wooden box. Staining the wood for a base color rather than painting over it allows the wood grain to become part of the design. In this project the frame is actually the predominant artwork with the inset artwork on paper acting as a continuation and complement to the overall design.

The crane image is inspired by an actual Southwest petroglyph design in Canyon de Chelly, Arizona, and the sun and tall grasses give an Asian feel. I love this combination of Southwest and Far East!

STAMP CARVINGS

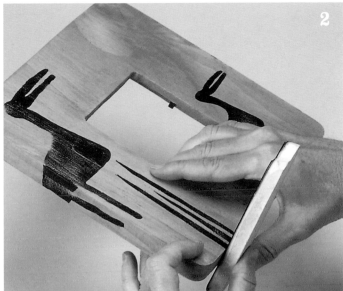

1 STAIN THE FRAME

Wearing protective gloves, apply the stain to the frame with a foam brush, then remove the excess with a clean rag. Let the stain dry.

2 STAMP THE BIRDS AND GRASS

Stamp the bird and grass images onto the frame, using the VersaCraft inkpad. The larger bird and the grass can wrap around the sides of the frame as well.

3 ADD THE SUN

Stamp the sun image in the top-right corner with VersaCraft red, and then go over it with the rust acrylic paint and a detail brush.

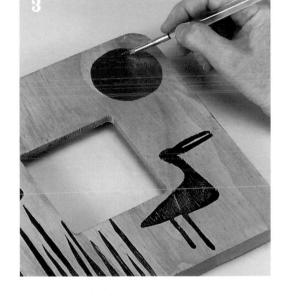

RETHINKING WOOD STAIN

HARDWARE STORES TYPICALLY HAVE A LARGE SELECTION OF WOOD STAINS IN MANAGEABLE ONE-QUART SIZES. THE OBVIOUS APPLICATION IS ON WOOD, BUT WHAT ABOUT PLAYING WITH STAIN ON PAPER? I LOVE THAT LOOK! I HAVE STAINED GRASS CLOTH, PAPERS FROM NEPAL AND ART JOURNAL PAGES. LOOK FOR THE WATER SOLUBLE VARIETY, SO YOU WON'T HAVE FUMES TO CONTEND WITH. WHEN YOU THINK "PAINT," CONSIDER WHAT MIGHT HAPPEN WITH WOOD STAINS, THEN PLAY.

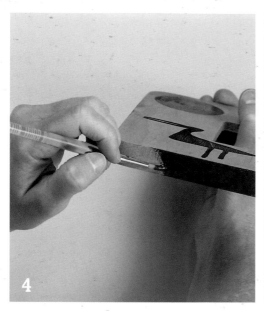

4   PAINT THE FRAME SIDES

Paint the sides of the frame with the rust paint, starting and stopping where the section of grass is stamped.

5   EMBOSS ONTO THE CARDSTOCK

For the artwork that goes inside the frame, trim the cream cardstock to fit the frame opening. Stamp the negative bird image onto the center of the trimmed cardstock, using the black ColorBox inkpad. Emboss the image with clear embossing powder and the heat gun.

6   ADD PAINT TO THE IMAGE

Paint around the image with turquoise and rust paint around the image. Then, place the piece into the frame to finish.

MULTIPLICITY

THIS PROJECT IS AN EXAMPLE OF THE JOY OF CARVING DIFFERENT SIZE STAMPS FROM THE SAME ORIGINAL DESIGN, SIZED UP OR DOWN BEFORE TRANSFERRING ONTO THE BLOCK. I ACTUALLY HAVE FOUR CARVED CRANE STAMPS; THREE ARE USED IN THIS PROJECT, AND THE FOURTH IS MUCH LARGER.

MATCHING BOX

This box started out as unfinished, but it is as easy to create as the frame. Follow all the same basic directions. Also, have fun inside the box! You can stain, paint, or add fabric or textured papers as liners. Découpage the inside with photos! Displayed together, the frame and box make a striking set.

ZEN SHADOW-BOX GARDEN

Create a personal, miniature Zen sand garden, using a shadow-box frame. My garden was inspired by the rock garden of Ryoanji Temple in Kyoto, Japan. Stain the wood black, stamp the surface, then add some sand and a minimal number of rocks. The rake can be bought in a Zen garden kit available at bookstores, or make one yourself by combining bamboo pieces.

97

WHAT YOU NEED

pencil

gourd, small to medium size

craft blade

craft saw

fine-grit sandpaper

paper towel

black inkpad (STAZON)

Decor it ink, black (RANGER)
(or substitute acrylic paint)

detail brush

template for carving provided
on page 124

NATURAL GOURD BOWL

Holding a gourd in your hands is an experience of nature and, for me, a way to touch ancient cultures and traditions. Gourds are as strong as they are beautiful in their sometimes wild uniqueness. No two gourds are ever alike. My approach in this project was to find bowl shapes with smooth qualities that are conducive to stamping. I love the natural color of gourds with the simplest stamp designs in black. My inspirations come primarily from African and Native American gourd designs. Someday I would like to add the element of woodburning techniques as an embellishment. Another class, another project . . . someday!

STAMP CARVING

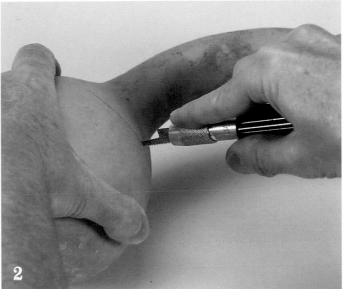

1 DRAW A LINE FOR CUTTING

With your hand resting on the table, hold the pencil securely. Rotate the gourd with the opposite hand to draw a continual line around the gourd at the spot where you want the top of the bowl.

2 SAW AROUND THE GOURD

Start a hole in the gourd with a regular craft blade, then using a craft saw inserted at that point, saw all around the gourd at the line. At this point, you can remove all the inside seeds and fibrous material. I use a metal spoon to scrape. You can soak the gourds in water to soften the material. Then wait until it is dry to proceed.

3 SAND THE EDGE SMOOTH

Sand along the cut edge of the gourd bowl until it is nice and smooth. With a damp paper towel, remove all the powdery dust left over from sanding.

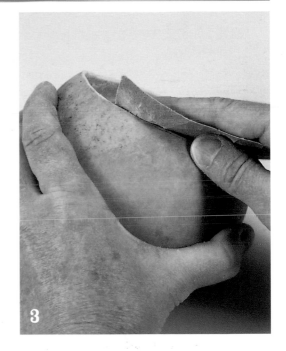

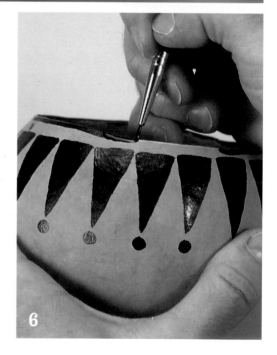

4 ADD A STAMPED PATTERN ☝

Stamp around the perimeter of the bowl. The surface of the bowl is curved and has some texture to it. Don't worry if the stamping isn't perfect! We are getting the pattern in place.

5 TOUCH UP WHERE NEEDED ☝

Touch up any missed spots with a detail brush and black Decor it ink (in a bottle). I liked the look of the ink so much that I basically went over the whole design with it.

6 FINISH WITH THE BORDER ☝

Add a small dot with your brush to the point of each triangle, for interest. Paint a small border of black around the rim of the bowl to finish.

LOVE YOUR GOURD

YOU CAN APPLY ORANGE OIL TO YOUR GOURD TO PROTECT IT, IF YOU LIKE. THE OIL ALSO GIVES THE GOURD A NICE SHEEN.

GOURD STAMPS
ON FABRIC

In Africa, calabash stamps are used to create the designs on different kinds of fabrics. I wanted to try to make a variation of those. I used a Dremel tool to carve some gourd stamps and used wine corks and the tops of small gourds to create handles, which were easily attached with a hot glue gun. The look when printing is primitive, and that's exactly the idea! This piece combines gourd stamps and carved blocks, traditional designs and my own innovations.

WHAT YOU NEED

flat bamboo sticks, two,
cut to 5" (13cm)

hot glue gun

hot glue stick

tin snips

craft glue

multicolored yarn

polymer clay, turquoise
{SCULPTEY III}

square clay cutter or clay blade

copper inkpad
{PEARL-EX}

mica powder, Duo Yellow-Green
{PEARL-EX}

template for carving provided
on page 123

OJO DE DIOS
ORNAMENT

Ojo de Dios means "Eye of God." Making Ojos out of yarn on sticks from trees was one of my first entrepreneurial adventures. I made and sold them in Santa Fe when I was in college. Start with two sticks, then advance your skill level to three or four, taking the basic Mexican idea and playing with bamboo and clay centers. My family has made dozens of them over the years, in variations galore! Try making one that is very large for a wall piece. If you do a little research, you can find books that will take you to three dimensions. For now, let's make little Ojos that make a big splash of color. Consider using slats from an old bamboo window shade as an alternative to newly purchased sticks.

STAMP CARVING

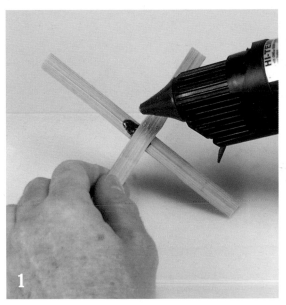 

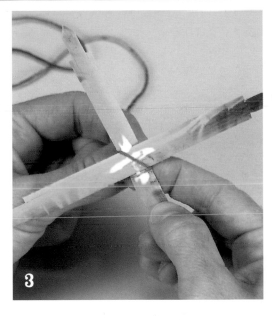

1 SECURE THE STICKS

Glue together the two bamboo sticks with hot glue, creating a cross.

2 NOTCH THE STICK ENDS

Snip bits out of the ends of the bamboo with the tin snips. Experiment with different cuts and patterns—it's fun! The bamboo breaks off in clean lines once you snip.

3 TACK ON THE YARN

Put a spot of craft glue in the center of the sticks, front and back. Attach the yarn in the back, and make one diagonal cross through the center, working with the yarn directly off of the skein.

CRAZY FOR YARN?

ONCE UPON A TIME, THESE ORNAMENTS WERE MADE PRIMARILY WITH A VARIEGATED YARN. THESE DAYS, FIBERS HAVE GONE WILD AND THE CHOICE OF FUN AND FUNKY YARNS IS IMMENSE. CONSIDER BUYING YARNS WITH FRIENDS AND SPLIT THEM UP AS AN ECONOMICAL ADVANTAGE AND TO GIVE YOU EVEN MORE VARIETY.

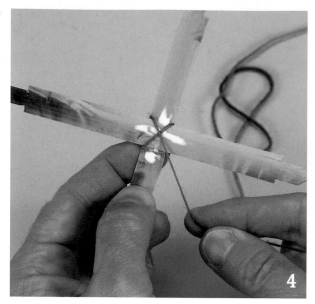

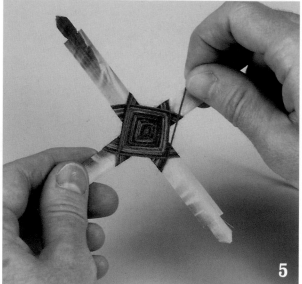

4 BEGIN THE WRAPPING

Bring the yarn around from the back and cross over, getting a rhythm going as you wrap around and around. Decide in which direction you like to wrap, and then wrap around each consecutive stick, turning as you wrap. A diamond shape begins to develop as the yarn builds up.

5 COMPLETE THE WRAPPING

Continue wrapping the yarn around in a counterclockwise fashion until you almost reach the snipped areas. Tack down the yarn with a dot of hot glue or craft glue.

6 CUT OUT A CLAY SQUARE

Condition a small piece of polymer clay and roll it out. Cut out a square shape with the clay cutter or blade.

7 STAMP THE CLAY

Stamp into the clay square with the stamp and the copper inkpad.

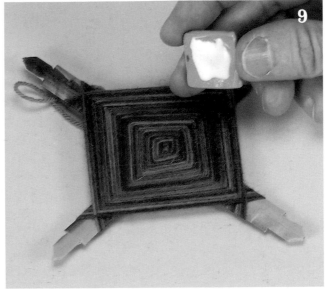

8 ADD MICA POWDER 👆

Using your finger, apply a bit of the mica powder over the stamped image.

9 ADHERE THE STAMPED CLAY 👉

Bake the square according to the manufacturer's directions, then glue it to the center of the ornament using a glue gun or craft glue. You can make a hanger for the ornament using a short length of yarn.

ORNAMENT
VARIATIONS

Using the basic ideas in this project, the variations are endless! You can use any kind of sticks—all sizes, stained or unfinished, standard shape or notched. Dowels of all sizes are easy to find and allow you to make really big ornaments! Use paint on the sticks for strong color. When wrapping yarns, have a variety of yarns handy. Simply cut off one color, add a touch of glue and start wrapping with a different color to get bands of different yarns. Get wild with the fibers— why not? Create nature-oriented Ojos by starting with sticks from a tree in your yard. In the centers, try punched craft tin for a Mexican feel. Add beads to the yarn as you are wrapping. Experiment with leaving space between sections of yarn. Key point: Have fun!

STAR ORNAMENT

Cutting polymer clay into basic shapes, with cookie cutters or cutting blades is easy. With just one star cookie cutter and one large hand-carved stamp of spirals, we can make a fabulous set of ornaments very quickly. We are basically rolling out the "dough" as we would for cookies. This is mass-production in the art world at its best. Each star is handmade; with creative applications of surface color, each stands out and shines in its own way. Try hearts and other shapes, too.

STAMP CARVING

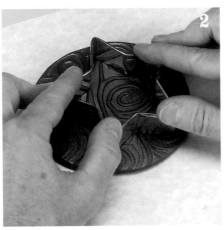

1   STAMP INTO THE CLAY

Roll out a piece of conditioned polymer clay to the desired size. Ink up a stamp with the copper inkpad, then press the clay piece onto the stamp.

2   CUT OUT A SHAPE

Cut out a star from the stamped clay.

3   ADD MICA POWDER

Add glimmer to the star using your finger and the Spring Green mica powder.

4   PUNCH OUT A HOLE

Punch a hole in one point of the star using a stylus or a wooden skewer. Punch from the front and then from the back for the smoothest hole. Smooth the hole edges gently.

5   ADD A BEAD AND WIRE

Bake the star piece according to the manufacturer's instructions. When cool, thread the wire through a bead and then fold the wire in half at the bead. Thread both strands of wire through the front of the star. Pull it taut, using your finger as a spacer to twist the wire for a hanger. Coil the ends with pliers to finish.

SEEING STARS

CHOOSING A THEME LIKE "STARS" OR "HEARTS"—YOU CAN FIND ALL DIFFERENT SIZES AND STYLES OF COOKIE CUTTERS TO GO WITH YOUR DESIGN THEME. CUT YOUR OWN AS WELL. IF YOU MAKE A CARVED STAR OR HEART STAMP, IT IS EASY TO STAMP THEM IN POLYMER CLAY AND THEN SIMPLY CUT AROUND THE EDGES. ARTISTS OF ALL AGES CAN CREATE THESE LOVELY ORNAMENTS AND FEEL PROUD TO FILL A HOLIDAY TREE WITH THEM!

WHAT YOU NEED

polymer clay, black and copper
{SCULPEY III, KATO POLYCLAY}

black inkpad {COLORBOX}

copper inkpad {COLORBOX}

hot glue gun

hot glue sticks

epoxy

black permanent marker

templates for carvings provided
on page 124

POLYMER CLAY "CHOP" STAMPS

I love my stone chops (official seals) from China and Japan and have commissioned several to be carved for me personally by a master Chinese carver. One is a massive stone with a Confucian phrase—"Words are the Voice of the Heart"—carved on it, in an old block style. When you stamp with these chops, you are transported to another time and place. For thousands of years, stamps have been used to seal immensely significant documents and have been the personal signature of great and sometimes infamous individuals. These chops will work great in all kinds of clay as well as in hot glue. Feel a sense of history in this project. Signed, sealed and delivered—with flair and a flourish.

STAMP CARVINGS

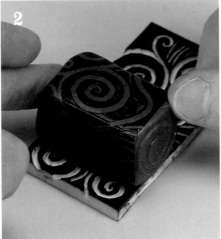

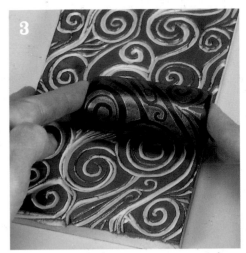

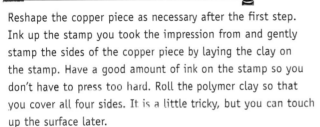

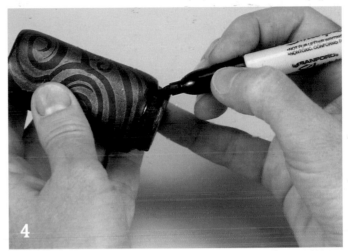

1 CREATE CHOP SHAPES ☞

Roll each color of conditioned clay into a chunky cylindrical shape. Flatten the sides of the copper piece into a square shape. Press the copper piece into the stamp. This creates the actual chop design that you will stamp with.

2 STAMP THE COPPER CLAY ☞

Reshape the copper piece as necessary after the first step. Ink up the stamp you took the impression from and gently stamp the sides of the copper piece by laying the clay on the stamp. Have a good amount of ink on the stamp so you don't have to press too hard. Roll the polymer clay so that you cover all four sides. It is a little tricky, but you can touch up the surface later.

3 STAMP THE BLACK CLAY ☞

Ink up the second stamp with copper ink and then roll the black clay piece over the stamp. Put a lot of ink on the stamp. Lighter pressure gets the ink on; heavier pressure adds texture to it as well.

4 ADHERE THE HAND-CARVED STAMP ☞

Gently stand the two rolled pieces on end and bake according to the manufacturer's directions. Because these are thick pieces, the time will be longer than usual. After they have cooled, glue a previously carved circular stamp onto the end of the black cylinder chop with epoxy. Color the white sides black with permanent marker to make it more attractive.

5 READY TO USE ☞

To use these stamps, ink them up with metallic pigment inks and set into globs of hot glue to get an old sealing-wax effect. The chop made with the carved block attached at the base can also be used on paper. The chop with the direct impression is a hard surface—it will be "interesting" on paper, but it is worth a try! Experiment on fabric, clay or other surfaces as well.

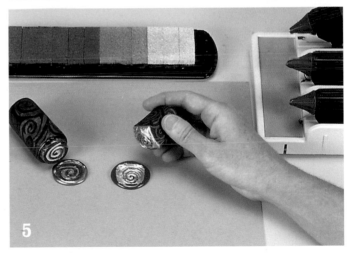

THE PORTRAIT GALLERY — ARTIST TRADING CARDS

A worldwide art phenomenon—**Artist Trading Cards.** These miniature works of art (2½" x 3½" [6cm x 9cm]) in any and all forms, make collecting "original art" easy and very affordable—they are never sold, they are always traded. Trading events happen in big cities and small towns all over the world. Artists who participate in art exchanges, many with themes or topics, amass great collections. How much fun is that? Welcome to The Portrait Gallery, featuring a spectrum of hand-carved images. Get inspired and try carving and printing your own!

ELIZABETH PARSONS

ROBERTA JAMES

DEBBIE KIEST

STEPHANIE CHAO

DEBBIE KIEST

NANCY DE SANTIS

DOROTHY KANSTEINER

NANCY DE SANTIS

DEBBIE KIEST

DEBBIE KIEST

DEBBIE KIEST

NANCY DE SANTIS

JANE ARNAL

NANCY DE SANTIS

DONNA HACK

DEBBIE KIEST

JANICE BRYANT

ROBERTA JAMES

111

THE MAIL ART GALLERY — CREATIVE CORRESPONDENCE

In this world of instant communication where e-mail has changed our lives, enter the world of mail art. It is timeless. There has always been something so special about a beautiful letter! How wonderful to open your mailbox, flip past the bills and ads and find . . . art!

ROBERTA JAMES

JANE ARNAL

JODY H SHIELDS

CARLA PATTERSON

JODY H SHIELDS

JANICE BRYANT

STEPHANIE CHAO

AUDREY LOUISE FISHER

JODY H SHIELDS

JENNY HUNTER GROAT

ROBERTA JAMES

KAREN LANDEY

JULIE HAGAN BLOCH

JULIE HAGAN BLOCH

KERRIN CONRAD

Whether a postcard or letter, an artistamp or stamped name and address, when there is a handmade element to the correspondence, we feel loved and inspired. Someone took the time to do this for me! Enjoy the variety and express your personal signature in new ways.

THE ART GALLERY

Offered in this gallery are the works of fourteen artists who were invited to create pieces using hand-carved stamps. No restrictions, just an opportunity to freely explore the medium and crank it up artistically. From the simplest carvings; beautifully rendered, to complex carvings and color palettes; from paper to fabric to clay and more, may this gallery be a feast for your eyes and an inner call to your creativity.

FIBER AND RAKU JEWELRY
SHARILYN MILLER (RAKU PIECES BY GLORIA PAGE)

PILGRIM II
JANE DUNNEWOLD

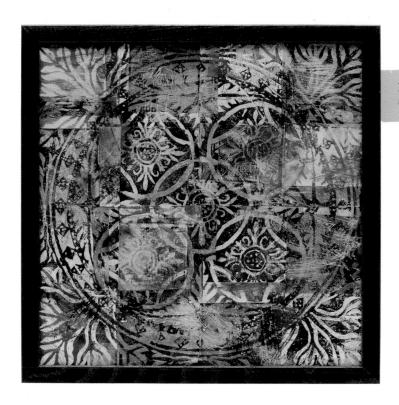

MOSAICO
MICHELLE WARD

ILLUSION
SHERRILL KAHN

115

NESTING INSTINCT
LYNNE PERRELLA

**BAI SHOU SHU
("ONE HUNDRED LONGEVITY BOOK")**
STEPHANIE CHAO

YOU ARE THE APPLE OF MY EYE
JO STEALEY

priests, beasts
And silk pajamas;
I think I'll stick
with two-l llamas!
Luann Udell

LLAMAS!
LUANN UDELL

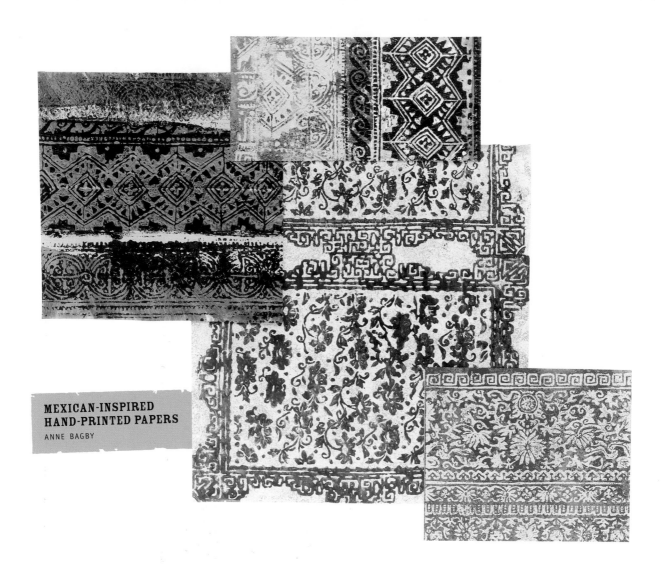

**MEXICAN-INSPIRED
HAND-PRINTED PAPERS**
ANNE BAGBY

**ARTIST TRADING
CARDS: FACES**
ANNE BAGBY

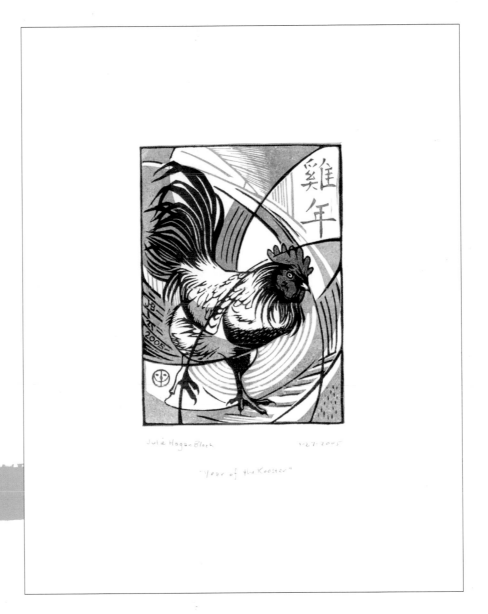

Julie Hagan Bloch   1-27-2005

"Year of the Rooster"

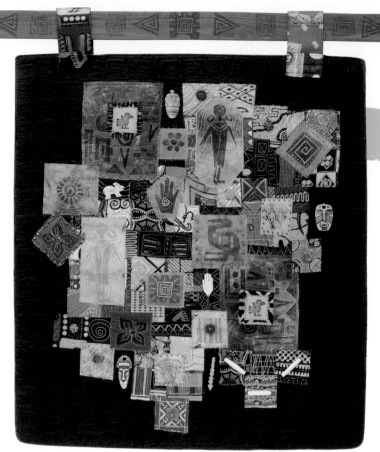

IMAGES OF AFRICA
JANET GHIO

APRIL'S SONG
LEANDRA SPANGLER

TEMPLATES

I am sharing these handcarved images for your personal use only (not to be mechanically reproduced and sold). Thank you for honoring that. The enlargement percentages will provide you with images that are approximately the same size as the ones used in the projects. Please feel free to size them up or down and use them as base patterns to carve your own stamps. Happy carving!

enlarge to 200%, then enlarge to 128%

enlarge to 200%, then enlarge to 132%

reproduce at 97%

enlarge to 200%, then enlarge to 125%

enlarge to 200%, then enlarge to 104%

enlarge to 200%, then enlarge to 109%

enlarge to 200%, then enlarge to 167%

enlarge to 200%, then enlarge to 179%

reproduce at 91%

enlarge to 200%, then enlarge to 111%

enlarge to 200%, then enlarge to 125%

enlarge to 200%, then enlarge to 156%

enlarge to 200%, then enlarge to 132%

enlarge to 200%

enlarge to 200%

reproduce at 95%

enlarge to 200%, then again at 200%, then at 139%

enlarge to 200%, then enlarge to 192%

enlarge to 200%, then enlarge to 172%

enlarge to 200%, then enlarge to 125%

enlarge to 200%, then enlarge to 161%

enlarge to 200%, then enlarge to 167%

enlarge to 200%, then enlarge to 179%

enlarge to 200%, then enlarge to 167%

reproduce at 99%

enlarge to 156%

enlarge to 200%, then enlarge to 132%

enlarge to 196%

enlarge to 152%

enlarge to 118%

reproduce at 87%

enlarge to 200%, then enlarge to 125%

enlarge to 200%, then enlarge to 125%

enlarge to 200%, then enlarge to 172%

enlarge to 200%, then enlarge to 156%

enlarge to 161%

enlarge to 154%

enlarge to 111%

enlarge to 200%, then enlarge to 192%

enlarge to 189%

RESOURCES

Most of the tools and materials used in this book can be found at your local arts and crafts or rubber stamp stores, but if you have any difficulty locating an item, contact these manufacturers directly for retail or online ordering information.

Carving Blocks & Tools

Dick Blick Art Materials
P.O. Box 1267
Galesburg, IL 61402
(800) 447-8192
www.dickblick.com
carving block, Thai Mango paper

Flexcut Tool Company, Inc.
(SlipStrop sharpening tool)
(800) 524-9077
www.flexcut.com
sharpening tools

NASCO Arts & Crafts
901 Janesville Ave.
Fort Atkinson, WI 53538
(800) 558-9595 (U.S. and Canada)
(920) 563-2446 (international)
www.enasco.com
carving blocks

Speedball Art Products
2226 Speedball Road
Statesville, NC 28677
(800) 898-7224
www.speedballart.com
*carving blocks, carving tools
and printmaking supplies*

Staedtler, Inc.
21900 Plummer Street
Chatsworth, CA 91311
(800) 776-5544
www.staedtler-usa.com
carving blocks, carving tools

Stampeaz
www.stampeaz.com
PZ Kut carving material, carving blocks

Inkpads & Rubber Stamps

Clearsnap, Inc.
509 30th Street
P.O. Box 98
Anacortes, WA 98221
(888) 448-4862
www.clearsnap.com
inkpads, MagicStamp blocks/sheets

Creative Chaos
Vickie Enkoff
www.vickieenkoff.com
alphabet stamps

Curtis' Collection
3326 St. Michael Drive
Palo Alto, CA 94306
unmounted Asian art stamps

Green Pepper Press
Michelle Ward
www.greenpepperpress.com
alphabet stamps

Impress Me Artistic Rubber Stamps
www.impressmenow.com
unmounted rubber stamp sets

OnyxXpressions
Cheryl McVeigh
www.onyxxpressions.com
Asian art stamps

Ranger Industries, Inc.
15 Park Road
Tinton Falls, NJ 07724
(732) 389-3535
www.rangerink.com
inkpads and reinkers

Tsukineko, Inc.
17640 NE 65th Street
Redmond, WA 98052
(800) 769-6633
www.tsukineko.com
www.tsukineko.co.jp (Japan)
inkpads and reinkers

Fabric Paints & Mediums

Jacquard Products
Rupert, Gibbon & Spider, Inc.
P.O. Box 425
Healdsburg, CA 95488
(800) 442-0455
www.jacquardproducts.com
fabric paints and inkpads

Dharma Trading Co.
654 Irwin Street
San Rafael, CA 94901
(800) 542-5227
www.dharmatrading.com

bleach thickener, Bleach-Stop, fabric art supplies

Polymer Clay

Polyform Products Company
1901 Estes Avenue
Elk Grove Village, IL 60007
(847) 427-0020
www.sculpey.com

Sculpey and Premo! Sculpey clays, tools and supplies

Prairie Craft Company (Kato Polyclay)
346 Brittany Drive
P.O. Box 209
Florissant, CO 80816
(800) 779-0615
www.prairiecraft.com
polymer clay and clay tools

Adhesives

Daige, Inc.
1 Albertson Avenue
Albertson, NY 11507
(800) 645-3323
www.daige.com
Rollataq Adhesive System

Uniplast, Inc.
616 111th Street
Arlington, TX 76011
(800) 444-9051
www.uniplastinc.com
hot glue systems and supplies

Collage Embellishments & Other Materials

Ichiyo Art Center
442 East Paces Ferry Road
Atlanta, GA 30305
(800) 535-2263
www.ichiyoart.com
Japanese and handmade papers

Painted Wings Studio
Dorothia Rohner
www.paintedwings.com
handmade soaps and bath salts

The Shoppe at Somerset
Stampington & Company
22992 Mill Creek Drive, Suite B
Laguna Hills, CA 92653
(877) STAMPER
www.stampington.com
alphabet stamps, Stacy Dorr glass tags and glass pieces

SkyBluePink
Christina Gibbs
www.skybluepink.com
beads, copper tags, Joss papers

Information Sites

The Carving Consortium
Soft Block Carving and Printing
Online Forum and Activities
http://theccforum.proboards9.com/
Linda Berman: unity@negia.net

Tyra L. Smith - Cloud 9
product reviews / information
http://netnet.net/~cloud9

The Gallery Artists

Anne Bagby
www.annebagby.com

Julie Hagan Bloch
Blochprint
www.peaceofmindproductions.com

Stephanie Chao
Cygnet Gallery Paper Arts
www.cygnetgallery28.com

Sue Nan Douglass
Paper Post
www.paperpost.net

Jane Dunnewold
Art Cloth Studios
www.artclothstudios.com

Janet Ghio
Janet Ghio Designs
www.quiltcollage.com

Sherrill Kahn
Impress Me Artistic Rubber Stamps
www.impressmenow.com

Sharilyn Miller
Sharilyn Miller ~ Fine Art Jewelry
www.sharilynmiller.com

Gloria Page
ImpressionsArt Designs
www.impressionsart.com

Lynne Perrella
www.LKPerrella.com

Leandra Spangler
Bear Creek Paperworks
www.bearcreekpaperworks.com

Jo Stealey
Jo Stealey Paperworks
www.jostealey.com

Luann Udell
www.luannudell.com

Michelle Ward
Green Pepper Press
www.greenpepperpress.com

I WOULD LIKE TO EXTEND MY PERSONAL THANKS TO ALL THE COMPANIES WHO PROVIDED ME WITH WONDERFUL MATERIALS, ART SUPPLIES AND VALUABLE INFORMATION TO HELP CREATE THE PROJECTS AND ART SAMPLES FOR THIS BOOK.

INDEX

127

STRETCH YOUR CREATIVITY EVEN FURTHER WITH THESE TITLES FROM NORTH LIGHT BOOKS.

CREATIVE STAMPING WITH MIXED MEDIA TECHNIQUES

by Sherrill Kahn

Over 20 dramatic paint and stamping recipes combine sponging, glazing and masking techniques with stamped patterns for outstanding creations. This book integrates traditional and nontraditional media in 13 step-by-step projects. Manipulate, decorate and combine different materials to create mixed media gifts and art objects.

ISBN 1-58180-347-8 paperback 128 pages 32315

RUBBER STAMPED JEWELRY

by Sharilyn Miller

This book combines the self-expressive qualities of rubber stamping with the elegance of jewelry making. Through easy-to-follow instructions and beautiful full-color photos, Sharilyn Miller provides all the invaluable tips and techniques you need to create earrings, necklaces, bracelets and brooches using a wide array of materials like fabric, shrink plastic and more. The book also includes 20 projects from the author and contributing artists.

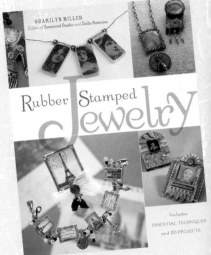

ISBN 1-58180-384-2 paperback 128 pages 32415

ART TO WEAR

by Jana Ewy

There's no better way to show off your creative talents than to adorn yourself, your family and friends with your own works of art. Whatever your unique style, this book shows you how to create jewelry, accessories and clothing that match your personality. Author Jana Ewy demonstrates how to dress up jackets, sweaters, t-shirts, flip-flops, purses and belts with paint, ink, metal, fabric, fibers, beads and even Chinese coins. You'll be inspired to make your mark on your clothing and accessories by the over 25 projects and variations included in the book.

ISBN 1-58180-597-7 paperback 96 pages 33110

FRESH IDEAS IN DÉCOUPAGE

by Colette George

Fresh Ideas in Découpage will show you how to create homemade decorative accessories that are infused with your personal style. Each project teaches you techniques for creating pieces with the layered and textured detail found in your favorite home décor shop but with tips and hints for making the piece your own. Inside Fresh Ideas in Découpage, you'll find over 25 step-by-step and variation projects that will help you turn your home into a show room. Each project will teach you simple yet sophisticated techniques, such as how to layer paint, wax, plaster, stain and even ink to create elegant finished pieces.

ISBN 1-58180-655-8 paperback 128 pages 33242

THESE BOOKS AND OTHER FINE NORTH LIGHT TITLES ARE AVAILABLE AT YOUR LOCAL ART AND CRAFT RETAILER, BOOKSTORE OR FROM ONLINE SUPPLIERS.